Midnight Ride Of The Son

1 Corinthians 8:6 Yet for us there is one God, the Father, from whom are all things and for whom we exist, and one Lord, Jesus Christ, through whom are all things and through whom we exist.

Midnight Ride
Of The Son

by

Kyle Walker

This book is a work of fiction. Names, characters, places, and incidents are either products of the author's imagination or are used fictitiously. Any resemblance to actual events, or persons, living or dead is coincidental.

Visit Kyle Walker at
facebook.com/songsofpoetryministrys

Joshua Holmes at
www.behance.net/Artman706 and
www.jahbookdesign.com

Printed in the United States of America
First Edition: September 2016
10 9 8 7 6 5 4 3 2 1
Copyright © 2016 by Kyle Walker. All rights reserved. Except as permitted under the U.S. Copyright Act of 1976, no part of this publication may be reproduced, distributed, or transmitted in any form or by any means, or stored in a database or retrieval system, without the prior written permission of the publisher.

All rights reserved.
ISBN 13: 978-1537612423 (CreateSpace-Assigned)
ISBN-10: 1537612425

Cover Design by Joshua Holmes

Dedications

Dedicated to Katelynn and Ilya, Daughters of Donielle, may my books help you shine with the rising Son

Introduction

Ever since the beginning of sin we have been lost, wandering in the dark. The Midnight Ride Of The Son poetry collection will take us on a journey across smooth and bumpy roads, with stops along the way. We need repentance and times of reflection while saving our children before the returning of the Son of God.

Two Girls

Hello how are you? By now you hold me in your hands
Like you always do before going to bed to read my poems
Well this poem you read now is for you

The Lord will be doing amazing things through you
Thanks to your Mamma for raising you the right way
Keep trusting the Lord through thick and thin

Two girls have never touched my heart as you two have
This is my way of thanking you for inspiring me like no other
Because of you my drive to keep writing will keep on going

The Lord knew the effects you will have in His kingdom
Thanks to your Mamma for loving you the way God intended
His ways will move you like never before

Two girls have never touched my heart as you two have
All the things I've gone through have been worth it knowing
The emotions felt to channel words to be read by you

The Lord knew why I needed to come into your Mamma's life
This Poet gets humbled every time I hear my poems have impact
All I try to do from my own little room is to make a difference

Hello now I bid you goodnight as you close me in your hands
I can only imagine the look on your faces as you read your poem
But I hope you two girls dream of making your own difference

40 Days

Know where I was, just don't know where I am going
Sometimes I get so lost in my wilderness that I wonder
As if I am doing my own 40 days of finding myself

We all have our own wilderness called life to wander
Some of us find a way out sooner, others take longer
Either way will come out changed better or for worse

Life circumstances tend to dictate where we want to go
Bad days we want to quickly end, good days to go on forever
Things happen out of our control and we don't like losing control

Even Jesus wandered in the wilderness, not to find himself
But to prepare Himself for what was to come, to endure sacrifice
Though tempted He stayed on the direction He was meant to take

God allows circumstances in our lives to mold us, mend us
We're not wandering lost as we might think in the wilderness
By following the path He wants us to take, He's helping us grow

Adrift

Innocents can only bring us so far from birth
Eventually our minds will open after our eyes
Will be seen alive while the soul starts dying

Adrift since birth born into sin where right seems wrong
The wrong feels right it's the way satan wants us to think
Only thing that keeps us from total confusion is emptiness

Puberty comes knocking at any age just matter of opening
Leaving the search for identity staring us right in the face
The exploration begins, the destination depends on the upbringing

Adrift since the moment innocents left us from birth
Eventually will wake up to the fact baptism is only water
No saving was done, just a public bath

Heart will open up to deceit as the void in the soul grows
Doing anything, searching everywhere to find something
That will keep us from feeling the death that is coming

Adrift to hitchhike until the stranger pulls over to offer a ride
Will there be enough love to bring back the moment of birth
As we look into the stranger's eyes to recognize who birthed

Innocence returns upon the second birth from redemption
Adrift no more, the soul satisfied with the Spirit that purifies
Now it's time to feed the fire that burns for the glory of God

Complex Simplicity

Looking in the mirror is lot of science that can't be explained without truth
Which is to admit evolving isn't possible not coming from a monkey to me
Only God could have created me to be me

The brain sends signals to the rest of the body to function
Yet stores every memory from sight, to smells, touch, feel
How can something like this be made by accident?

Only do we humans make everything so complexing
Yet it's the way God made us, with a curious mind we use
With the free will we choose that is exploited by the devil

The heart is the biggest muscle that pumps blood for survival
Yet at the same time can be the downfall of our own destruction
The heart is deceitful above all things, desperately sick from sin

Only do we make truth so complexing with the lies we tell ourselves
Why we think we'll be satisfied with anything, but what we can't buy
Yet only the simple truth will only satisfy our hearts desire

Science can only take us so far in explaining how we got here
Or how creation was in desperate need of a Savior to save us
Only faith can see the truth beyond our understanding

Looking in the mirror gives me complex thoughts of how
Jesus chose the wickedest place to live inside above all
Yet the simple truth, because He loves me satisfies

Circles And Frustrations

How long do we keep stepping in the same footprints
Until we realize just going in circles over and over again?
Then frustrations will begin trying to find the way out

Pain can be steps back, keeping us from where we need to go
But can also be stepping stone needed to get over the wall
The hand of God is reaching to pull us over

How many signs do we need to pass until we stop to realize
They all point in one direction, but we keep going our own way?
Before we know it, hell comes into view, think it's too late

Hurt of the heart can be different kind of pain that keeps us apart
But it can also be the difference that brings us closer to the Healer
Just have to open up let Him in and will be saved

How many good deeds will we do till we realize not working
Nothing we do will get us any closer to finding away outta here?
Not until we recognize the sin committed is keeping us apart

Circles And Frustrations will be our downfall unless we humble
While on our knees, accept the one direction given which is Jesus
Only then will we find the grace which has given us the way out

In To The Night

Birthed into darkness we came even when the sun shines so bright
But it's hard to see anything when being born into the black of sin
It's like living in an underground world with no sun

Just hard to see the truth when nobody else shows us any different
Not when surrounded by those that say it's okay to keep on sinning
Not that they know any better themselves

If only somebody, anybody would shine their light even like a firefly
Just long enough for us to see the whole new world being missed
One light seen can draw them closer to the truth they need to see

The church used to have candles lit for those wandering in the night
With a door always open to give rest and answers to those seeking
But someone blew the candles out and locked the door

If only the fireflies that light up the dark skies would light together
Or better yet churches come together in agreement for once in Christ
Light back up the candles, be the light of the dark world Jesus commanded

Yes we're birthed into darkness until shown the way into the light
So we can be born again, only this time with a spirit to show us truth
And recognize the voice that calls into the night until we come home

The Potter

There was this Potter that could make anything out of nothing
One day decided to make something different, something unique
So He went and got the best dirt for making clay

Sitting at the spinning wheel, pushing down with His foot got the right speed
With His gentle hands started to shape the clay into a shape like no other
His helpers even stopped to see what He was making

A minute only passed by but to the Potter felt like a thousand years
But slowly He molded the clay just the way He wanted without flaws
The smile on the Potter's face showed how proud he was of this creation

The Potter having to step away to get some more clay, a jealous helper moved in
Who took it and threw it into a deep black hole and it broke into a million pieces
Oh how the Potter cried in disappointment but climbed into the black hole

Picking up the pieces putting them in His water to soften back to clay
With some blood mixed in water His creation started to make shape again
The flaws fixed, looked good as new

The Potter holding up His creation smiled and said it is finished
He said I will never let you out of my sight, day or night you're mine
With that said He began to paint His creation

Whys

Frustrations of this world we all got them little things, big things
Yet still they shouldn't get to us, we should know they don't satisfy
So why do we have so little backbone against world's lies

Whys are the questions we ask while searching in boos and cigarettes
Because we think it relieves the pains and stress from lack of understanding
While taking it out on those around us, related or strangers, the sin is the same

Don't let things of this world distract us so much we forget why we're here
Should be living in rented cabins instead of building mansions for ghosts
Why build to stay when we're only passing through?

Frustrations come from backward priorities, not putting God first
When we place God above all, even when it means selling everything
Save the soul, lose the world to gain the understanding we seek

Answers to the the Whys will never be found in this world
Not when we need to understand, to accept the answer of truth
Only when we accept Jesus as the living Word will we be satisfied

Whys will come and go which will never know the answers to
But long as we have Jesus, truly follow Jesus, shouldn't matter
If we truly trust our Lord and Savior, will be full of joy not frustration

Time To Kneel

Days aren't getting any longer, just getting darker as time flies
Excuses are wasted words swept away by the wind like dust
We all have something to offer that will light the way

Doesn't matter where we are, what we're doing we can stop
Not even time itself can interfere when we're being called
The time to kneel and pray is now in Jesus's name

Age's number doesn't matter, youngest to oldest we have the will
That God our Creator gave us before becoming a seed in our Mothers
We can use this will to call on Him no matter what is happening

No matter where we are, what we're doing even to our last breath
Not even if death is staring in our faces, death has been defeated
The time to kneel and pray is now in Jesus's name

Short or tall, nothing to do with same gender or color, sin don't care
Only thing Sin cares about is burying us in an avalanche of darkness
All started by a little white lie served up by satan the lord of darkness

If there's any time to kneel and pray in Jesus's name it's now
Pray for His blood to wash away our sins, pray for our family
No time to waste when it comes time to kneel and be saved

Days are getting numbered backwards, not forwards like time
Excuses to not Believe are words being swept away by the wind
Jesus will return and when He does time to kneel will be over

Upside Down

World we live in must feel like the biggest pit thrown inside
Until we get sold into slavery owned by the prince of darkness
Who is waiting for us to break down and curse God out

This must have been how Joseph felt when he was betrayed
But like Joseph I will use this time on my knees to my advantage
Will wipe that grin off satan by praising the mighty name of Jesus

The world we live in feels like a snow globe at times
That we're trapped inside and satan is shaking us around
Just waiting for us to break down and curse God out

This must have been how Job felt when He lost everything
But like Job I will use this time on my knees to my advantage
Will wipe that grin off satan by praising the mighty name of Jesus

World may have us hanging upside down till our pockets empty
Satan is a big bully we let push us around until we fall on our faces
Just waiting for us to lose favor with God for cursing Him out

This was until The Son of God came down born from a virgin
Walked the earth for 33 years kicking satan's butt until the cross
Satan tried keeping Jesus down, but can't beat resurrection power

Jesus holds the world in His hands we just view it upside down
Satan has no control over us unless we give it up through sinning
No need to curse God, no need to blame just learn to praise Him

This was until Jesus started writing in the sand saying sin no more
Let us use this down time to thank our Savior, talk to Him, praise Him
Satan stays away when we're praising the mighty name of Jesus

Angel Inside

Some don't realize what's inside of them until it's too late, Or if they do try to hide it behind their own cloud of doubt Except from the one that looks through the eyes into the soul

Everything seems to crash around us nothing goes our way no one believes in anything we do so why should we believe? Will be better to think we've failed at everything than to hope

How can anything be good inside of us when we live for the world but the world lives against everything we do just spins till we fall except the One that created everything and sees everything?

So how can anything be good inside if we don't even believe it's in me? Someone please tell me, anybody at all tell me why should I believe if the ones we love don't believe in me why should I believe in myself?

Just when we think all is lost the light comes through the cloud of doubt And the Light says I am the Christ that died just to show the world not only, oh not only to show the world my love for you but my belief in you

Don't we know when Christ is inside us we're the light of the world? No darkness can blow this candle out like an angel's light it glows Not just a saint but an angel that shines for the Lord's return

Don't we get it yet an angel lives inside of you that's what I see inside looking through your eyes into your soul the sparkle is an angel's light, the world doesn't have to believe for it to be real or for you to see

Just have faith and believe this is a message from the Christ our Lord who just wants you to believe what He's telling you is true, so true before birth an angel was put inside us all He's inside you now

Psalm 139:14-16

Angel Of The Night

Point of no return not even words will come to pass this moment
Despair now lives in my eyes that looks up in the brightless moon
Though it's full the eclipse hides the hope that now cries tears of blood

Falling star empty thoughts won't make wishes tonight luck's run dry
Even if you'd hit me wouldn't feel anything just feel the glowing light
That gets brighter the closer it gets widening my eyes

A freight train coming down from the sky only seeing the light in the tunnel
Should I run away or except my fate meeting head on letting the fear be gone?
With arms stretched out eyes closed I await the gates of hell to open

Embracing kiss of death wasn't that of steel but that of the flesh
Instead was a kiss of life that came from arms of flesh out of love
The blood on me wasn't mine but was His with arms stretched out

No falling star, no light from a train just blindness in seeing the truth
Quick to fear what we don't understand in the answers from questions
Falling into our own trap that only leaves a window of hope to look for

Point of no return not even words will come to pass this moment
Dirt torn nails cling to the fingers that hold the bars in the window
Looking up in the night eyes, not stars stare back into mine

Falling Son of God from Heaven to earth not to bring me wishes
Only to give new life that's free from Terrene's darkness of eternity
Leaving the window of hope only to return through the door He holds

Angel in the Night came when all was lost no point of return not even words
The moment was passed long ago, the only hope was the eclipse of the cross
Shedding His blood so that we may stand in the light of His glory who is Jesus

Born Of This World

Yes, we're born into this world but does that make us experts?
Just because we walk the earth, sift dirt through our fingers, see
The birds fly in the sky, gives us claim to make the age of existence

Just because we have eyes with 20/20 vision doesn't mean we see
An eagle can see a rabbit run on the ground way up from the sun
It's not just what we see, but how we see the truth

This world isn't ours even if we're born onto what we don't understand
The darkness blinds us with greed things we can't control yet consumes
With bitterness and hate towards the truth which would free us

Yet before birth God the creator knew our first words before a breath
Born into a world filled with darkness the Son of God gave light to see
But then the light surrendered to the darkness of our sin on a cross

So the world thought three days later the Son came out shining light
Darkness still consumes the world giving blindness to those that see
In that darkness an eternal light can be seen by those that can't see

Yes, we're born into this world in passing not as rulers but slaves
Those that follow the light will be set free seeing with new eyes
Everything the Light touches will be seen with eagle eyes

Born of this world we are but like a caterpillar to a cocoon except
We're not butterflies but eagles of the night giving light to the world
This is the vision we get seeing with the heart of God

Bridge To Heaven

Hearing John 3:16 we would think be enough for us to see the light
But for most it's not enough, a picture is needed to paint the truth
So we paint the story of love the best we can yet it's not always enough

Angle upon angle we try to get everyone to understand what we see and feel
Black and white, then color thank the Lord story of love can be told many ways
Even tried putting the cold truth on the big screen but some thought was too harsh

Close the eyes of the flesh, open the eyes of the heart let these words be felt
Pretend we're walking on roads upon roads all leading to this one crossroad
Yet no matter which way we turn come to road's end to a ravine

This ravine is narrow yet too far to jump across, when we look down see lava below
On the other side is a big stone blocking a gate with a sign in front with these words
Only those without sin and have the key may pass into the promise land

Just when we give up and realize no other way but have a leap of faith to cross
Out of nowhere, a Man appears before we leap and says wait I will build a bridge
So He gathers two pieces of wood, lays them across the ravine, yet too narrow

Taking three nails took rope off His back to make rails for us to hold then laid across
Then He said if we believed He would hold the bridge together to walk across but please
Would we lay our burdens down on Him to make the way complete?

With the sacrifice we walked across the bridge, with each step felt burdens lifted
Hands of forgiveness had taken them as we took the last step across this bridge
Looked up in time to see the stone roll away, to see on the other side to see Him

Couldn't help to look back found the human bridge gone, just a bloodstained cross
That was all that remained, now look into the eyes of the One who made the way
The scars in His hands, his feet and side clearly visible like a key in a door

Now all we have to do is turn the key called Jesus open the door walk on through
At the same time some how the door to our hearts open now feel his hand in hand
As one, walk into the light, the darkness has now faded away, gone forever

For God so loved the world He gave His one and only Son as a bridge to heaven
Whoever believes could walk across lay their burdens down so they can be lifted
Through forgiveness the key to open the door of eternal life is opened walk on through

Now open the eyes yet feel Jesus hand in hand tugging to walk with Him
Together feel the darkness flee letting only His light remain shining with love
No longer viewing with eyes of the flesh now we see with eyes of grace

Broken Dreams

How many of us have traveled these roads called dreams to find them fade away?
All our childhood we wished to be, only to find we're the villain instead of the hero
Just like there's broken roads, there's broken dreams

Chasing these dreams so many times leads to broken relationships, loneliness
The only thing we see beside us or over us is our own shadows, which reminds us
We're alone to drown in our despair, blinded by our own self-pity

So what do we do give up not only stop dreaming but tell others don't believe
And some times those others happen to be our kids their future they fail to dream
After all our dreams were broken, so lets make them live our broken dreams

Chasing these dreams so many times lead to our misery as our look-a-likes fail
Once again our dreams fall apart, as our children grew up fell upon their own dreams
The problem is we're still seeing our shadow as self-pity and not giving our blessing

Broken bread, was a broken body that hung on a broken dream from which we drank
Yet it wasn't my dream, so why does it matter if someone died to make my dream real?
Wait a minute, what did I just say? The Dream Maker broke His to make mine whole

Chasing this dream so many times led to many lasting relationships, everlasting joy
The shadow we thought was behind us, turns out was not ours, but the Son of God's
Problem was instead of looking down, should have been looking up

Sometimes before dreams come true, must be broken then made new again
No dream is born perfect just like we're not born perfect from the sin of our Father
Doesn't mean we should stop dreaming our own, just stop living theirs

These broken roads lead to fixed dreams, these broken dreams lead to fixed roads
What is now broken will be made new, just like when we get born again with Christ
The Dream Maker now lives in us, we're living His dream which makes ours perfect

Sometimes the broken dream that we wanted doesn't turn out the way we planned
Only to find out the dream wasn't what we were to be living, but who was to be living
The once-broken dream has now given birth to a new one of love given from a child

Caileigh Cloud

There's a cloud overhead that's far away, yet getting closer
Don't know whether to run away or run toward the cloud overhead
Could a storm be on the horizon or something beyond my thoughts?

The cloud is getting closer still not sure what to make of it or what to do
My mind is telling me to get on my horse and ride like there's no tomorrow
But my heart is telling me this is more than what meets the eye

Cloud is close enough to hear now not sure if it's thunder and lightning
Or if it's trumpets mixed with a harp and sweet voice from heaven on high
My mind is really racing while my heart is feeling the breath of heaven

The cloud is almost on top of me there looks to be a twist like a finger
As if pointing I want you to take a ride with me that will be a knee shaker
Will look like two hundred miles an hour, but will feel like a snail's pace

The color in the cloud is just splendid like the colors of heaven color of love
Honey cloud is that what you are not a storm cloud but a cloud of love
Bringing a shower of love from the throne in heaven above

Caileigh cloud are you heaven-sent, riding on one of the King's chariots?
My mind's made up I'm getting on my horse, listening to my heart's cry
Let's go ride until Heaven's cloud returns then will go up together as one

Now that my mind has cleared, my heart has stopped the pounding
The eyes of my flesh have closed so the eyes of my heart could open
The rainbow's hidden treasure is breathtaking never knew a way in

No wonder I was so lost in trying find you the rainbow's hidden treasure
Was so busy running to find the pot of gold at the end of the rainbow
When all this time the treasure is inside the rainbow chasing me

One Concept

There are sixty-six books in the bible but one concept
That we're consistent in failing to grasp or simply forget
Out of all the books they all lead to one simple concept

In Genesis we read we're created in six days in paradise
Everything we need or could ever want we had right there
But we failed to grasp one concept and wanted more

Even after the fall God tried telling us through Abraham son Isaac
But all we saw was Isaac laying on the alter and the test of faith
The ram should have given the concept away right then

Then of course there's Moses freeing God's people and the desert
Forty days till being led to the promise land yet still failed to grasp
The concept God was trying to tell them

Queen Esther's story should have given us a clue but no
We still try and carry everything on our shoulders including
The world that is not ours to bear, but His who is to come

Yes we know Job lost everything and that we should trust the Lord
Through everything we go through, but we still end up asking why
Through all the questions we let the concept slip right by

Shout with a joyful noise the Lord just wants to hear our praises
Psalms teaches us and that He knows the words on our tongue
But still even though He knows us we fail to know Him even in praise

The prophet Isaiah tried to tell us loud and clear with His stripes
By His stripes we're healed but know somehow slipped by
Like a quiet wind guess we really do need a hurricane to feel it

Three times a day Daniel prayed no matter what even in a lion's den
The concept should have been known then but we took praying as
A requirement instead of a privilege talking to our Heavenly Father

Shadrach, Meshach, and Abendnego inside the fiery furnace
We once again failed to see the concept and see the fourth man
Just seeing once again not to bow down to anyone but God

So seeing we needed the biggest clue of all between day and night
God gave us John three sixteen sending His Son to die on a cross
Just to give us the one concept we failed to grasp

Even Jesus tried to tell us before His walk up the hill to save the world
Through all the miracles only a few grasped the concept even the thief
Got the concept, which so many of us fail to grasp

Finally even through the resurrection we're told the concept
Through Paul's letter to the Corinthians, faith, hope, and love
The greatest of these is love

God wrote sixty-six books through His spirit to tell you and me
Just one thing with one concept in mind that we find so hard to believe
All our Heavenly Father wanted us to know was I love you

God tried telling us it wasn't just about obeying His laws, but us accepting
His unconditional love trusting that love and knowing His love is our shield
After all that, all He wants to know is one concept in return, Do we love Him?

Earth's Spinning

One bucket that's all we see of the earth's waters
Compared to the view of God's who is the creator
Even the astronauts will tell you there's no comparisons

The picture of earth from space on TV doesn't do God justice
Unless we turn from the lies of Darwin and believe the truth that
Jesus is Lord and in the beginning He created the world

One handful of dirt that's all we see sifting through our fingers
Compared to the whole earth being held in the hands of God
Even when we hold the plastic globe there's no comparisons

Take a look in the side window mirror, objects appear closer than they really are
This car we ride in called life we tend to drive too fast, missing the turn of salvation
Breaking down isn't all that bad someone has to put on the brakes

What's the point you say with the creation and life's car ride? Well take off the glasses
Put on God's 3D shades to see the world's not blue and green like we see it, but black
Like oil blackness of sin leaves sludge that corrupts anything it touches

How many views of the world, of God's salvation do we need to see truth?
That there's no comparison there's only one Creator, one Savior in Jesus
Only one held the world in their hands as He died for us to see His view

Earth is spinning in His hands made from His breath of spoken words alone
Just get to see a small sample, breath a small sample the beauty of perfection
Question is, Will we have Jesus breathing in us before earth's spinning stops?

Eyes In The Sky

Every single thing we've done or haven't done has been witnessed
Though no soul is seen with human eyes, we're never truly alone
Not every eagle can be seen from the ground, but He sees us

No clouds or darkness can keep His eyes from seeing our every thought
Let alone the secrets buried deep within our hearts, His eyes see everything
Like He promised we're never alone, never out of sight

Look up in the sky can we see, eyes in the sky looking down at us
Let us lift up our hands in thanks, and praise, no need to shake in fear
These are eyes of love not of judgment, those eyes will come later

Every single thought or word spoken will be heard from ears unseen
Every eye in the sky will have ears connected to them with a mouth
With a trumpet at their lips, ready to blow for the Lord to hear

Are those stars we see or angel eyes of God looking down upon us
His protection is all around us, not just from evil, but from ourselves
Still leaves it up to us to seek His will for the way in or the way out

Eyes in the sky see everything, with ears that hear everything
Just waiting to see our hands up, voices crying out for Him to come
Praises of His name will be the thanks needed for His help

Don't we hear His voice calling out of the dark, making light to see?
Angels will be the witnesses as the world only hears thunder, lightning
While heaven's angels party, celebrating our saving

Eyes Of Your Heart

Open up the eyes of your heart to see the holy truth
Close your eyes of the flesh to stop seeing the lies
The time has come for no more questions

The eyes of the flesh only sees what it wants and nothing else
Blinded by greed and deception of self-righteousness leads astray
Without the light of the heart only leads further into darkness

Open up the eyes of your heart to see the holy truth
Close your eyes of the flesh to stop seeing yourself
The time has come for no more questions

Forget the image in the mirror if it distracts from the real purpose
Look into the living waters to see the real you and live free of doubt
Don't let the ripples of reflection pass you by without knowing

Open up the eyes of your heart to see the holy truth
Close your eyes of the flesh to stop seeing eyes of death
The time has come for no more questions

Close your eyes of the flesh open up the eyes of the heart
See the man with scars in his hands, He was nailed down
Died on a cross to close the eyes of the flesh to sin

Open up the eyes of your heart and see Christ knocking
He walked out of the grave so that the eyes of your heart
May see the truth so that death has no sting for eternal life

Open up the eyes of your heart to see the holy truth
Close your eyes of the flesh to stop seeing the lies
The time has come to drop the questions and follow

Fear Of A Flash

Sitting here watching the news seeing, hearing about the two-car crash
Hairs on my head start to tingle, fingers start to twitch, hearts pounding
Oh no! What if that could have been me or someone I loved? Oh God no!

Fear of a flash in our minds of the future that might or might not happen but
Too late the devil's trap has been sprung fell for the lie now we start to panic
Part of us reminds us of God's truth, of control, the other just wants to drown

As I lay me down to sleep start thinking about tomorrow if it ever comes
Surrounded by darkness look out the window even more black with no moon
Getting hard to breath, heart's pounding again, Oh God could this be the end

Fear of a flash in our minds of the future that might or might not happen, but
Our thoughts have turned into racecars speeding two hundred MPH in our mind
God's truth has become the speed limit sign that we only see for a flash

Found out tragedy has struck in the friends, family for once has come true
Now I am lost for words when I see their face or think of them what to do
Oh God what can I say to someone that's lost a child?

Heart's pounding, sweats streaming down my face, hands shaking, thoughts racing
Feels like ten thousand miles though just pacing back and forth no closer to answers
Visions of all that's happened keeps playing over and over seeing all the hurting tears

Fear of a flash in our minds of the past about two thousand years ago yet feels today
See vision of a cross with eyes in the sky looking down with hurting tears falling down
The Father above has just watched the death of His only Son in the name of love

Three days later Mother Mary felt her hairs begin to stick up, heart began to pound
Found the tomb of her Son open but He's no where to be found just a pile of rags
Oh, God she began till an angel appeared and said fear no more He has risen

Flash of a cross in our minds knowing the Father holds us in His hands through Christ
Who held us in His arms in the time of our greatest need and holds us forevermore
What do we say to those that cry hurting tears? Fear no more He's risen with Christ

Forget To Breath

Sometimes we get so caught up in what's happening around us
That we not only start living the world, but start to breathe carbon dioxide
The poison of the world that causes us to black out of faith

So let's not forget to breathe inside out the breath of Christ that flows
We don't need to breathe the stress of the world that tears us down
Just that of Christ, which will be our eagle wings to fly higher

The world is full of darkness that sin has consumed us long ago
Only those living in this sin will be blinded to the truth of why the death
Not knowing sin the demons have possessed have no problem of massacre

So let's not forget to breathe inside out the breath of Christ that flows
We don't need to breath the worry of the world that makes us doubt
Just that of Christ, which will be our shield, our strength

The cancer that's consuming our flesh lives off the world's carbon dioxide
Doesn't have to overcome ourselves, preservation of living in the word of God
Can't breathe both the world and that of Christ, love and war don't mix

So let's not forget to breathe inside out, no longer breathing in the world
Christ came down to die on the cross letting out His last breath for us
No longer do we have to breathe the poison of the world, just that of Christ

Sometimes we get so caught up in what's happening beside us, through us
That we forget about living in the world, stop breathing, that makes us weak
Long as we don't forget to breathe that of Christ, we will fly higher like an eagle

God In the Midst

For those that still think Christ is still dead from way back when
Didn't see Him come alive before the people of west Papua Indonesia
The hand of God came out as if to say, Here I am take me now

The Word of God is alive the language spoken doesn't matter
Like the river that began from a tiny brook, flows into the hearts
Before we know it they're waving palm branches

Even though we may yet to understand their language, we understand them
As their voices shout and sing Jesus Loves the Little Children our language is one
The Kingdom of Christ has cast out another shadow of darkness

Their prayers now can be heard even though we're continents away
Once again our tongues, their tongues though different speak the same
The revival in the land is alive, spreading like wildfire

For those that know Christ is alive, waiting for His trumpet return
Seeing the hand of God in the midst of these people bring praises
Because it's written when the last will be saved He will come

The question remains who the last will be, so why take the chance?
The Gospel will reach the last of His lost people soon so don' t wait
What if the last man lost in the jungle gets saved, leaving you behind?

The Word of God is alive, the Kimyal are living proof He speaks
Let us join in waving palm branches, singing Jesus loves us
In every language we become the living Promise of God

God's Diary

This book was written by the One that sees everything past, present, future
So call it a book of fairytales if you wish because I believe in fairytales then
I also believe the author of this book is the God that came down to save me

Think what you want, believe in what you wish, but will know the truth
Sooner or later oh how the truth will be known how God stopped time
Not just time but gave His only Son just to say He loves you and me

This Book was written by the One that created heaven and earth in six days
Don't we get it yet, He knows what heaven looks like for what it really is worth
But also has seen the cost of rejection the destruction that hell makes

This Book is more than sixty-six, but a map into the unknown unseen danger
That the darkness of satan hides so well the perfect place to set unseen traps
But through Christ we can walk through this valley of death without fear

Love letter some call this Book, I also believe it's God's diary to better understand
The confusion comes when we forget our thoughts our ways are not His way amen
For His thoughts, His way is perfect, beyond measure, the only understanding we need

Doesn't take a brain surgeon to know this book of healing cures all diseases
Even heals the broken heart that's fallen into millions of pieces don't give up
The Lord holds the pieces in His hands, He will make things new

Thank you Lord for writing your words down then speaking them to me
For now I know how our first family lived so that history wouldn't repeat
If only we could learn to trust and obey we could live forever too

Wouldn't the scientist be stumped if we started living in the hundreds again
Just like Noah did or father Abraham, now we just think it's impossible to do
That's because we forgot what it takes to trust and obey God's Holy Word

Miracle Of The Impossible

Thousands of churches start praising, worshipping at the same time
Here the time zones have disappeared as millions of voices are heard
The presence of the almighty God is felt He is seen in each place

How is this possible? we ask, well just like the seven seas connect
Even though water surrounds land the waters of the world connect
Doesn't take science or logic to know God has no bounds

Thousands of hospitals with millions of dying people starting to live again
One hand touched each one at the same time the doctors are speechless
The questions are endless yet at same time don't know which to ask

How is this possible? we ask, well just like the lightning stripes the sky
The power is felt in awe as even though a split second the night is lit up
The glory of God is felt for an eternity what we don't see is the connect

Millions of people are lost around the world waiting to be found again
Don't be afraid as the ground starts to shake an the wind begins to blow
This is just the Rock crying out, the Rock's voice being heard, being felt

How is this possible? we ask, well just like each sparrow even in millions
They each have a home to go too, so do the lost even if we don't see them
Everyone will have a chance to know that the Rock Christ Jesus loves them

Billions of people pray even though they doubt they'll be heard without answers
I admit I am one of them as we forget and wonder where God is in this big world
Worst yet we question whether God is bigger than our problems when they're so small

The problems only become so big when our trust in the Lord becomes so small
How Great is our God Whose love even overflows the oceans drowning our doubts
Even greater is our God's understanding and forgiveness in grace and mercy

Thank you Lord for being you as your love your glory in the light shines in the world
The only darkness is that in me, so I ask the glory of the redemption of your blood
Create in me a clean heart, like the millions and millions with me, make me one in you

Millions and millions still don't get it, they look around mocking those that believe
Even though angels too many to count dance around them the party so big in heaven
The joy of the Lord overflows down to earth as the believers' voices in praise can be heard

How is this possible? they ask, Well the world may seem crazy but truth is
The world is just on fire for the Lord and the devil's reign has come to an end
Christ the King is coming for His throne then everyone will see Him face to face

Radiance

Looking into the dark mass we now call space was nothing but water
But the radiance seeing through the eyes of the Beholder was perfect
No planets, no gas to cause big bangs, bringing dinosaurs to extinction

Just like a painter looking at a blank canvas seeing His masterpiece
What nobody sees except the first angels that worship Him in service
The first fog of breath, producing light that separated darkness

Looking into the dark mass now mixed with light saw that it was good
Making the light day, the darkness night until evening became morning
Still no planets, no gas to cause big bangs, just angels seeing first day

Just like a painter admiring His work so far, thinking what to paint next
What nobody sees except the first angels is the grin on His radiant face
Then one-by-one, day-by-day what was once nothing became living art

Through the Creator's eyes we see the creation of heaven and earth
Then Land came between the oceans, soon came, plants and animals
The sun and the moon, stars glowing of the Creator's radiance and glory

Looking through hands we see nothing but dust seeping through fingers
But the radiance brings out our form before we knew it had a face and body
And for the first time saw His face just like a Father looking at his firstborn

What we didn't see was the day we'd fail to see His face with the first sin
Never saw the shake of His head until it was too late then only saw shame
Who knew how long it would take to see the Father's face again?

Through the tears in His eyes we see the Creator, master Painter's radiance
All wasn't lost the perfect plain became work of art the Creator became created
Except on this canvas became a living sacrifice for all the world to see

Now what we didn't see before, we now can see through the living Son of God
That this once dark mass we now call space, now light between heaven and earth
Is now the radiance of His undying love that we will see on our Father's face again

Voice In The Dark

Can anyone hear me from within this dark hole
Try crying out but sounds just like a bullfrog
Instead of seeing the Voice in the dark

Looking up as if at the bottom of the well that's caving
The air is bad enough now the walls begin to collapse
So now a Voice in the dark scratches just to be heard

Like a water hole in the desert that holds water for a time
But quickly evaporates becoming dry, leaving no sign of life
Just a voice in the dark that only a horny toad knows

Noise that's loud drowns the thoughts that channel down the wire
Can't think to hear, can't think to speak just a Voice in the dark
Though they hear me, can't hear my own Voice in the dark

Many random voices called thoughts inside my head, which to listen,
Which to use, how to say them without confusing them being stuck
Till then a Voice in the dark sifting through, thoughts that confuse me

Seeing them look down at me from this dark hole, well that's caving
Though they want to reach in to help, but draw back not knowing how
Hard for them, hard for me, so our voices stare from within the dark

Voice in the dark, meant to be in the light, will anyone hear the cry?
Breathe the air to push the walls back, bring the clouds that rain holy
Living water that comes from the Son, making a Voice in the rainbow

Why The Boy

There were five thousand maybe more if they had family
They were gathered waiting to hear to be healed by Christ
Yes we know the story with the bread and the fish

But out of all the men that were there, why did it take a boy?
Christ asked Philip how to feed them who was counting coins
Only a boy understood what Christ was asking

The boy followed the crowd probably out of curiosity not knowing
But He heard the call of Christ and with child like faith believed
Doesn't take a wise old man to know that Christ is the bread

So again I ask, Why did it take a boy to feed the five thousand?
So often we hear move on from the faith of milk to meat we chew
Yet out of all the carnivores took the faith of a child to listen to Christ

Could it be we underestimate the bigness the power of Christ?
Are we crossing our fingers every time we pray in hope of receiving?
Don't be caught counting when Christ the King is giving you the keys

Turn on your child like faith don't toss it, don't lose it, just use it
Yes build your faith stronger but no need to replace faith of a child
Like building a house, instead building a house of faith

Christ is asking you, How will we feed all the hungry people
Will we be saying we don't have enough while counting coins
Or will we be the boy and say multiply what I have and believe?

Tug Of War

Amazing what we hold with sentimental value in this day in age
That we just can't let go of, yet not satisfied, always wanting
Yet still refusing to let go with what we got in our hands

We pray to God, give me this, give me that, with arms full of junk
Don't we realize we're no longer living on milk, but eating meat
Past the age of toys and games, we're needed to work our craft

Fancy gadgets have us lost in a dead end canyon of no real value
While relationships that we held dear suffer until we find ourselves
Smart devices can't replace heart-to-heart, eye-to-eye communications

All is well with what we got, until we lose what we hold dear
Then we become mad at the world, blame God for everything
When we could have spent more time if only we'd let go

Don't we know by now God takes what we have for a reason?
So He can give something, or someone that will make us better
After all, He is our Father and doesn't want to see us to hurt ourselves

Tug of war is what we're playing with God over a lake of fire
We think we're pulling on rope, when in reality it's our death
What we're holding is sin and we need to let it go to Jesus

Amazing what we hold with Jesus and He should be held on High
After all, when we gave Him our sins, He gave us His love to hold
And His love has many hands to hold those we want to love

Tug of war I am done playing with God, to Him I give everything
Gaining everything to help me reach for those I need to find again
So I have the leverage to tell them, let go to reach He that saves

Wild Horses

There's nothing like riding through the country on horseback
Brings a whole new view of the Creator's glory and Master's touch
How sweet would it be if just me and God were riding the trails?

Wild horses run along God's green earth, happy and free
Look up from taking a drink from the still waters, give thanks
They listen for His voice in the wind, whinny with praise

Riding on horseback into the wilderness might run into these horses
Look close might get a life lesson watching them run free without worry
Not only see God's beauty at play, but look deeper will find more

Like growing in faith must spend time with them get closer
When you do they will be your best friend will come when called
Just like spending time with God, more we do, the closer we get

Saddle up, let's ride, give them their head, don't worry about the size
Some may look small, some may be spottie, but don't underestimate
The heart will carry you on when trails get rough, won't let you down

Broken Roads

Broken roads we'll travel until we come to the crossroads
When we have to make the decision on where to go next
Do we go for the smooth blacktop or stick with the broken?

Coin flip or leap of faith? Luck of chance or ask directions?
Usually comes down to the patience and guidance received
Would be wise to pull over and read the map God's given

Smooth roads will only take us so far even deception fades
Just as roads give way to potholes, the truth reveals secrets
Both will cause damage if driven over too fast

Stormy seas, broken roads, it's all a part of life given
Whether sailing or driving both need a Captain, not us
Jesus needs to take control of the wheel

Broken Roads we'll travel long as Jesus is driving
Direction doesn't matter, only those that need fixed
His Love will fix everything He touches

Leap of faith is handing over the keys to Jesus
Trusting Him to take us where He wants us to go
Jesus is the map God gave us to follow

Chip Away

Life is full of heartaches, pains that go deep into the heart
If we don't deal with this pain properly it hardens the heart
It's why we must let it go on through

Not all is lost when we let the walls come down and give access
I know the heart's been broken more times than not, but its okay
Good times, good memories, are still ahead coming our way

Lies will hurt when we believe them instead of the truth God has given
But the truth will still reveal faults and weaknesses that will carry pain
The pain will ease as we hand them over to Christ

The Lord will chip away at our hardened hearts until we fall to our knees
Doesn't matter what is protecting our hearts, He will find a way through
Even if it means taking us to our limits, His love will be felt again

Life is full of second chances, which is ours for the taking when we let go
Because we can't take anything when we're full of bitterness from pain
Only way to feel the joy again is by letting it all go in the hands of the Lord

The Lord may take a hammer and chisel or melt us back down into clay
He will chip away and mold us back together piece by piece till complete
This is what He will do when we're broken, He will make us new again

Twisted

Each dream began with me holding a shovel digging a hole
The first time I thought I was digging for buried treasure until
I looked around found myself standing on Boot Hill then woke up

The next dream found myself holding that shovel digging again
This time thought I was digging for a well until found myself back
Standing on Boot Hill beside a tombstone with my name

Woke up in a cold sweat the smell of dirt was too real to be a dream
But my boots were clean no dirt under my nails but still too afraid to sleep
Had to make some coffee to stay awake forgot to look if I made decaf

Shovel in hand started digging away like there was nothing else to do
Thought I was digging a grave to bury a fallen friend, but couldn't move
Found myself waist-deep in dirt that I was still piling on

Dream took another twist found myself holding the shovel inside the grave
Throwing the shovel laid down found eyes looking down at me from above
Instead of feeling fear felt calm as the face became clear it was me

Three days later found myself being helped out by a hand of a stranger
Step-by-step started walking down a long and narrow road with no end
But I knew long as I followed this stranger wouldn't have to dig anymore

Feeling the sun shine on my face got up and out to get the paper
Waved to my neighbor who gave me a stare that I wouldn't forget
He asked, Were you digging last night? as he pointed to the shovel

Ventilating

Sometimes news from this world can be so suffocating
With all the violence, killings and threats of terrorist strikes
Sure does make it hard to breathe in this polluted environment

Global warming won't matter if we don't stop polluting ourselves
What we're taking out of the earth isn't what's killing us, it's sin
The earth didn't commit the sin that spread the darkness, we did

Sometimes the gossip in the social world can be so suffocating
With all the lies we tell, make up, bullying one another, for what?
Sure does make it hard to breathe in this white lies of a world

Outlawing guns won't matter if we don't wake up and repent as a nation
Put God's word back in schools, put the commandments back on courthouses
We need to put back the Man of God around the dinner tables

Turn off the TVs, put away the cellphones, open up the Bibles
We could save ourselves, if we devoted as a family to humility
With one family at a time loving like Christ

Church and state has suffocated America for far too long
We need God in every school, every big house, every home
Surrendering to Jesus Christ is our only hope for ventilating

Confused Nation

How did we allow ourselves to get so confused on who we are?
What magic mirror did we look into that had us decide it's not me?
Was there nobody to show us the truth of whose we are?

When did we start neglecting the teaching of moral truth to children?
Shame on the parents if they did the same to you, but don't be blind
Leaving out the truth, from thinking no harm, no foul in their innocence

How did we allow ourselves to get so confused on what we are?
Who gave permission to experiment on our moral values God gave?
Satan may have given the hint to try, but acting on them is on us

The moment we decide to keep God on the shelf instead of hearing Him
This is when we started neglecting the teaching of moral truth to our children
We stopped deciding what is best, while allowing opinions to become their parents

Sins of the parents shouldn't be on the shoulders of our children
Shame on the church for staying on the sidelines, not getting involved
Someone needs to take God off the shelf, listen to the truth He speaks

Judgment will come for those playing god instead of obeying the True God
Who's calling for our repentance before becoming another Sodom, Gomorrah
They too thought very little of the wrong in their innocence too late

Blame is our own for becoming a confused nation with our neglected moral truth
For keeping God on the shelf, even the church ignored spoken error of our ways
Take the Bible back off the shelf, start the revival of being set free

Oh God, forgive the neglecting of not only hearing your truth, but obeying
Unbrainwash us, so we may repent of our sin that keeps us from grasping
Set the nation free by setting me straight with Your truth

Afraid To Be Broken

Nobody wants to go through pain or suffering
That's the part of life we'll go through questioning
But will never understand the answers given

We're too afraid of change, being people of habits, routines
So we fight with all our might against lack of understanding
We'll even go far as killing the answer we don't like even if true

When we suffer sickness we think, how can a God allow it to happen?
Not understanding free will, and the deception of the devil being real
Instead of seeing God's glory at work, we choose to blame

Nobody wants to go through, or see pain, or suffering
We still wish to be stronger without lifting the weights
Life doesn't work this way, got to go through

Don't have to be afraid to be broken, afraid to change
Won't go through alone, God will be with us working
Because when we're being broken He's up to something

When we suffer pain or sickness God is using it for glory
And when God's glory is being seen, lives are saved forever
All the while we're getting stronger in faith

Don't be afraid to be broken, don't be afraid to change
Might not understand the answers given, but trust Jesus
We're not the only ones in need of healing

Deeper Than Our Belief

The bite of forbidden fruit goes against more than God's say so
Adam and Eve couldn't see how deep the root of evil was implanted
Or the domino effect sin causes one after another

If God's love is deeper than the ocean, then how deep, how vast is sin?
When sin separates us from the love of God to the point of damned eternity
Which God knows when He forbids us of anything

Color of skin has nothing to do with the hate that builds within
The arguments we come up with are pointless, like the solutions
Until we accept the truth of which we don't understand, we'll fail

Until we see the devil pulling our strings, we'll do what we want, when we want
He will feed lies into our ears of "since we don't understand can't be true"
While we get deeper in the darkness of sin, with each sin committed

Demons are real inside our heads as we commit mass murders
While the world is recovering from the shock that brings confusion
Seeing everything but the truth, not wanting to believe the unexplained

Until we get to the root of all evil that's in each and everyone
We'll fail to get past our lack of understanding and stop sinning
Until we accept the fact we don't have to understand to believe

We never saw the falling star from heaven which was satan
We weren't there when satan took a third of angels, now demons
So never knew the serpent that God knew as we took that bite

Thank you God for not giving up on us from a lack of understanding
Even when we failed to listen with our trust your love runs deeper
Thanks to your sacrifice on the cross in Jesus I understand salvation

Whoever sees Jesus dying on the cross for their sin in repentance
Even though was over 2000 years ago, we can proclaim to be there
Will be saved, as Jesus Christ is living through us today

Dead Alive

Saw a stranger reading a newspaper, asked what he was reading
Said about you in the obituaries, looked and there was my picture
Every detail of my life before my eyes

Heard Jesus calling my name while He was dying on the cross
Said Father forgive him doesn't know what he is doing while dead
Every sin I committed was coming out of His blood

Saw a Medical Examiner standing over me asked what he was doing
Said performing your autopsy, looked into an overhead mirror, there I was
Every inner detail of my life, what was there, who was missing

Heard Jesus calling my name while He was knocking on my door
Said remember how I died for you, but didn't stay dead out of love
Every bit of my shame I felt was being lifted, but still doubted

Saw a Mortician getting a viewing ready for a memorial, asked who it's for
Said it's for you, time to get you ready, there I was looking at my own casket
Every photo of me was on display with every person I touched

Heard Jesus calling my name while standing inside of my door, hands out
Said feel my nailed, scarred hands, no need to doubt just let me in to stay
Every part of my being came alive as I was filled with His love

Saw hands reaching into a birth canal, asked who was being born
Said it was you, just as I felt a slap and woke up, seeing for first time
Never felt more alive than when I accepted Jesus Christ into my life

Ephesians 2:1-10

First Snowflake

Sometimes we feel left out, that somehow we've been forgotten
Everyone would rather talk to the popular, the main attraction instead
So we sit in our own little corner, watching the rest pass by

Just like the first snowflake falling that no one remembers as it melts
Only the big and final flake gets remembered as the snowstorm ends
But the first snowflake was just as important as the last

God remembers, the first star made in space, first grain of sand placed
Above all, remembers every one of us placed on this earth first to last
Just like the first snowflake we all have high value in what we do

Sometimes we feel not needed, or important, but rather a burden
Just because we're not as tall, not as strong, or not functioning right
Though we still try our best to fit in, just never feeling good enough

Just like the first snowflake falling that only melts on impact
Though it tries its best, only impacted one little spot for what?
Certainly nothing worth remembering

God sees our first breath, to our last, knows our first to last of many
And God used every one of them to make, do something wonderful
Everyone matters, every little thing matters in God's eyes

There's a first to last in everything, someone had to go first
The first snowflake is just as important as the last snowflake
We just need to believe in ourselves enough to be the one

KYLE WALKER
Grace Calling

Loss of life of those we loved can take us down a journey unknown
Much as we try preparing for the storms that might come unexpected
Somehow always end up forgetting, regretting what we left behind

Easy for us to lose our way with our heads down, eyes won't see
Not when our hearts are frozen to the point of not feeling anything
Will thaw out with the warmth of love, which will help us hear
If we look up long enough will hear grace calling, saying come back
I know it feels like the sky is falling, the world is crashing down, but
Jesus still has His arms stretched, holding your world in His hands

Times of moving, that brings on change that makes letting go hard
Even to the point of needing to pry our fingers to letting them go
No need to feel regrets, they know, they understand, they love you

Truth will always be there to set us free when we stop resisting Him
When we're free will see grace waiting to take us where love is felt
That is when will begin to feel the tingling of love mending the heart

Grace will keep calling until we listen to the voice of truth saying
Everything will be okay, you're losing nothing, only gaining victory
I am grace and truth, but you may call me Jesus, anytime for anything

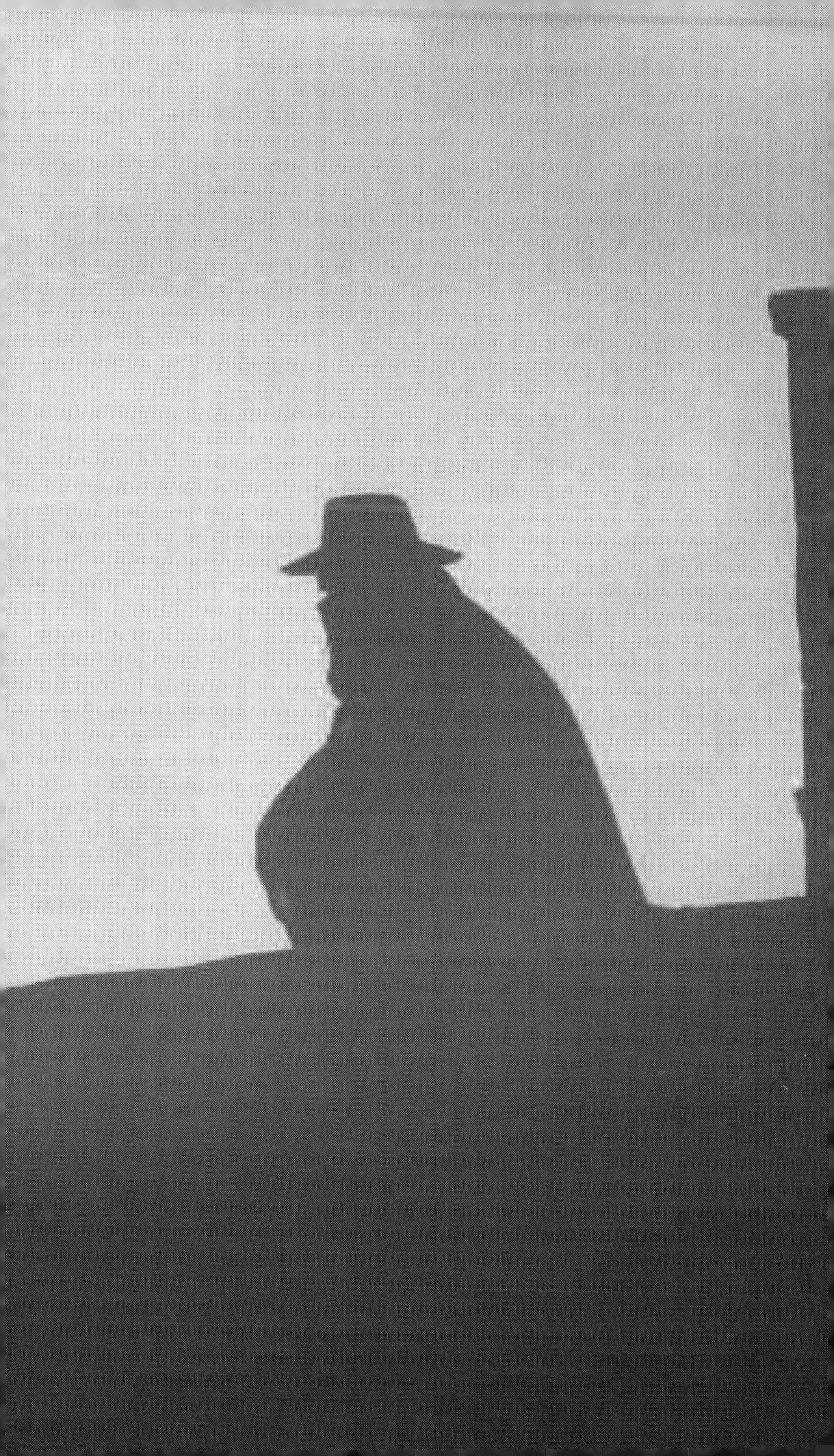

KYLE WALKER
Electric Faith

Trials of faith will come and go, pass or fail
But those that pass will build perseverance
So that we lack nothing

Those without faith will struggle when death comes calling
This is why we need those with faith to step up to fight for them
They need to know how faith can give them hope

We may never know the reason why we're chosen least expected
Though it's a given one out of one will pass, never knowing when
Why we can't keep Jesus waiting outside our door, let Him in

Those with faith need to show how passing the test is done
Show how God will give wisdom to those that ask with no doubt
That these tests aren't meant to punish, but to prepare for the journey

We may never know the mission for our calling until face-to-face
But God knows all, sees all who need us, to show them the way
Some just need the extra encouragement to press on

Well death came knocking at the wrong door opened by doctors
But faith struck back at death with the word of God, not my time
Jesus says faith has made him well, chasing death away

Those that just witnessed God's miracle, maybe even first time
Felt their own heart beating again thanks to your electric faith
Now they too have the faith to slam the door on death like Jesus

Clouds of Comfort

Clouds hang over my head, feels like they'll never leave
Only matter of time till a rain pours down that won't stop
My mind wonders if the Son is gone, but heart believes

Might not always feel, or see His work at hand
But I know He's there with me just as He promised
Boat may be rocking, but He still commands the sea

When we cry, we don't sorrow alone, no matter whose pillow
The cloud may be hiding the moon, but His tears can be heard
Just as they pound on our roof in harmony of our hearts beating

Might not always feel the hand that wipes the tears away
But I know Gravity has a name, Jesus will wipe every tear
His Spirit will comfort our hearts, just like He promised

We'll prevail through every hardship because He knows
We're strong with His strength, we're chosen for His purpose
Because the Lord knows others follow that are weak

Clouds hang over my head, feels like they'll never leave
The rain may come at any moment, but the Son still shines
Every beat of my heart is a praise as my sorrow is vanished

We may never understand why we carry thorns in life
But will be comforted to help those in need of comfort
God will give us comfort in all that we go through

Always Be

Doesn't matter what's before me or behind me, even if it looks impossible
The Lord will always be with me, taking care of the worries that haunt me
Even if I break down in a total wreck, He will be there to pick me up again

Storms in our lives will come and go, avoiding them is out of the question
Damage will be done, faith will be tested, but the Lord will get us through
And the Lord will be with us to pick up the pieces, making us stronger

Doesn't matter who's for me or against me, even if they look impossible
The Lord will always be with me, taking care of the worries that haunt me
Even if I pull all my hair out He will pick them up, put them back in my head

Life will be going good till we walk in quicksand, then we will begin to sink
The more we struggle trying to get out on our own, the deeper we'll sink down
But the Lord will always be there waiting for us to take His hand

Doesn't matter what happens to me, makes me stronger or weaker even cancer
The Lord will always be with me, taking care of the worries have lost control
The Lord will always be in control and in Him I will place my trust

A New Dawn

Only one knew the life meant for us to live and that's the Creator
He knew our being before our seed, before this life was ever planted
Even knew the twists and turns we would be taking to get here

The thing is we're not His puppets, but His children with free will
We need to move our own two feet, choose our own actions to fate
Even with things that happen out of our control

Darkness surrounds us, tests will be taken without knowing it
But with Christ there will always be a New Dawn on the horizon
She will inspire us to keep fighting, to live through body and mind

Beach body will just be one of many platforms of fitness reached
A New Dawn will be on the horizon within each of our hearts to rise
Thanks to Her walking testimony, we're inspired to move inside out

Through sweat and tears a New Dawn was risen by the miracle given
Even though clouds of rain may come, will go to the max or refresher
Knowing the Son will come through with the rainbow shakeology

Skeleton

Six feet under beneath a tomb unknown lay a skeleton of a corpse
Laid to rest long ago yet can still see the scars that the skin bared
The persecution of this Christian is still visible, though only bones

When living this Christian walked this earth with no worry of tomorrow
Time didn't matter even as days passed, with Him time stood still, as if
Not even death could stand in His way

Walked by this Christian everyday seeing the persecution yet not believing
Never did we lift a finger to stop the persecutor even though blinded to see face
The signs were very clear even though hiding behind lies

The zebra that lays with bloody rib bones showing flesh and skin attached
We see what was a Lamb now a Lion after the slaughter we failed to believe
Quickly do we forget satan was an angel now fallen

The Christian now a skeleton of a corpse laying six feet under tried to warn us
Yes we wish it's all good with love, that there's no devil, no apocalypse coming
So what's the point in scaring everyone from behind the pulpit?

Instead of paying heed we ignored this Christian since we didn't believe no one did
Threw stones for our gratitude, slapped His nail-scarred hands away that reached out
Could have been, should have been saved if only we listened to our hollow hearts

Six feet under beneath a tomb unknown lay a skeleton the eyes start to glow
Flesh, blood start coming back as new breath fills His lungs bringing life back
The resurrection of this Christ now complete, no longer a Christian

MIDNIGHT RIDE OF THE SUN

The persecution of this world isn't against me but He that is Jesus Christ
Because the world hates Jesus Christ so does the world hate me in Christ
The world will leave me a skeleton beneath a tomb unknown

Greater is He that is in me than he that is in or beneath the world that hides us
That forgets even in the darkest pit will be like light to me for the sun isn't needed
The glory of Jesus Christ shines through this witness that rises

Sun and the Moon

Take marbles in your hands then look up at the sun and the moon
Faraway looks small yet at this distance only see the edge of truth
Big and bright giving us so much light from the hidden danger

The closer we get to the sun the hotter it gets will even blind us
Too much sun we burn, too little sun we go pale, get cold in life
Being placed in the third rock from the sun is no accident

Whatever the troubles are, no matter how big they are, just remember
Instead of putting our heads down at night, crying ourselves to sleep
Look up at the moon, imagine the Lord holding it like the marble

The moon is so big and bright only the darkness of earth stops the glow
Without the moon there wouldn't be any tide that cleans the oceans of love
It's the sun and the moon that gives us life third rock from the sun

Whatever the heartache, no matter the hurting pain we go through
Instead of putting our heads down at night, crying ourselves to sleep
Look up at the moon and know there's nothing that can't be cleaned

The Lord didn't only create the sun and the moon with His breath
But He also holds them in His hands to show there's nothing bigger
Great is our God holding the sun and the moon in one hand like marbles

Just before sunset can see both the sun and the moon kiss us goodnight
Giving us a closer look at the distant truth in one hand of God as the other
Hand grips ours just a little tighter to let us know He's holding us too

Shadows

I can feel the sweat trickle down my back in middle of winter
The day might as well be nighttime too, the shadows so dark
Can't even tell when nighttime ends and morning begins

Know what you're thinking, How can there be shadows without light?
You will know what I am talking about, sadly enough down the road
Life can be full of regrets, leaving you left in wonder, what if?

Restless at night twisting and turning of endless thoughts of past
Wrong choices still haunt me day and night with no end in sight
The guilt pours in me like a leaking faucet

Everywhere I go someone always brings up my life's mistakes
So I thought in my mind, Even though they never spoke to me
Taking one look at them reminds me how I hurt them

These shadows follow me everywhere, no hiding, no running
Oh Lord, if you're there, raise me up above these shadows of mine
Through your sacrifice I know I've been forgiven, so why the quilt?

What's that Lord, I need to forgive myself before you can raise me?
But Lord, I don't know how, show me so these shadows will leave
Oh Lord, let me lean against your cross, let me use your light

Shadows leave me now, I am under the cross of my Lord
His light leaves no shadows, His light conquers every shadow
In His light of the cross every shadow is forgotten

Legacy Lives On

With every passing of those that we love how do we reflect on our own life?
How do we compare to the one that's going to be laid to rest till Jesus calls
Except that body's empty, just a hollow vessel, their legacy still lives on?

Don't we understand that's what they would want not to get bitter or drown in tears?
That's how she went to be with Jesus face-to-face full of smiles and overflowing joy
And now she still stands with Jesus, smiling full of radiant light that shines down

So how do we go on living without the ones we love beside us each and everyday?
That's when we need to start reaching within for the truth, stop reaching for the lie
Though it hurts the pain is still real, the truth will set us free

They're still here just like Jesus is no longer in the tomb from two thousand years ago
Oh no, Jesus is alive in us, through us, and now the ones we love are with Jesus
So now they too live within us, through us their legacy lives on

Don't stop living just because they have broken free from the grips of this world
They have left their legacy behind so that we may carry on giving hope to others
That the love of Christ will set you free from the chains of this world of darkness

So how do we compare to the one being laid to rest today till Jesus comes back?
We don't, but live the life she would want us to live, which is in love through Jesus
This is who she served, this is the legacy living on, one person at a time

With every passing of those we love day-by-day, step-by-step, heart-by-heart
Before we know it this legacy that lives on is now coming through the clouds
Now we too have left the legacy for others to follow as we go home with Jesus

Eye Of The Moon

Looking up into the eye of the moon can't help but wonder
If it's the eye of the Heavenly Father looking back down at me
And what He is seeing me and what He saw in me to choose me

Seeing the shadows in the light of the eye of the moon can't help
But wonder if that's what He meant even the darkness can't hide
Even in the darkest shadows the eye of the Heavenly Father sees

Still looking up into the eye of the moon can't help but wonder
What did the eye of the moon see way back two thousand years?
After all the eye of the moon has been seeing since day one

What was it like to witness your own birth to the world you created?
What was it like seeing your own face kissed by the mother of you?
Was your eye of the moon teary eyed seeing what was to come?

Eye of the moon did you close your eye to the beatings to your flesh?
After all the miracles just a few days before you saw yourself give
Now you're seeing them chant 'crucify' to your Holy Name

I know eye of the moon you saw the future the worth of this sacrifice
Seeing your flesh upon a cross nailed down with a crown of thorns
Are you thinking about all the sins or the day that crown will be of gold?

For three days eye of the moon you saw what it would be like without
A living God, I can't help but wonder what that would have been like
But then I shutter looking up in the eye of the moon and thank you

Raising up my hands as if waving up at the eye of the moon in praise
There's not one word I can say feeling thanks isn't good enough for coming
I hope giving you my life is enough for saying thanks for coming back Alive

Looking up into the eye of the moon can't help but wonder time and time again
If it's the eye of the Heavenly Father looking back down at me and what He sees
Is He looking into the future again and seeing when He comes back for me again?

Echoes From The Mountain

Whispers in the wind some may say but not the eagle soaring above
Who flies higher than we could ever see beyond the clouds, blue sky
No clouds in the darkest of storms can stop the vision on this eagle

What the blue sky hides beyond the clouds is a mountain like no other
The only way to get there is through the rainbow of eternal salvation
But like an avalanche the message of the mountain echoes down

Carried by the wind this message comes except one time in a virgin
That conceived through the spirit of the mountain giving birth to a King
For 33 years this Living message walked the earth till His sacrifice

Like water evaporating into the sky the King went back to the mountain
Before He left spoke of His returning and listening for His echoes of hope
Just like the rains restoring life so will His eternal love

Echoes from the mountain rain down like singing angels above
Those that recognize the King's voice will feel His eternal peace
Those that never knew him will just feel windchills of buried sin

Whispers in the wind some may say but not the eagles soaring above
Who flies higher than those left behind will ever see beyond the darkness
The glory of the King will be all the light these eagles will need

What the darkness tries to hide beyond the deception is a mountain
The only way to get there is through the Rainbow of the eternal Christ
But like an avalanche the message of the mountain echoes down of love

Country Roads

Sometimes we have to forget the highways and byways
Start taking the long scenic routes along country roads but
Take your time, no use speeding otherwise miss the point

Far too long now, we have been speeding down through life
No wonder we have forgotten how to live this life free of worry
When we let our brains slow down, will begin to understand

God didn't make us to go one hundred miles an hour a second
Yet we go that fast twenty four seven, no wonder He slows us
Otherwise we crash and burn blame everyone, everything we see

I know the country roads look dry and dusty but only to the fast eye
Take the hint, slow down, look out the windows, see God's creation live
Sometimes have to pull over and take notes of the lessons we learn

When we slow down might see the deer in the meadows without worry
If summertime the kids playing free as they know God is watching them
With squirrels chirping in the trees even the birds join in the praise of song

Don't we get it don't you get it yet if not need to slow down even more
Maybe when the rocks start crying out singing praises talking praises
The good Lord doesn't care which way, just wants our praise of thanks

When we start living free in God's beautiful creation, with no thoughts
Or worries flying, just seeing in awe for the first time what God has done
The hanging jaw open mouth will be praise enough now that you know

Time stands still when we praise the Lord with all our heart and soul
All of God's creation knows even if they live for a moment with praise
The moment can last forever in the name of Christ who saved us

Blood and Water

There was a man that stood on a hill long ago with his arms stretched
Claiming he loved the world, to prove it he did miracle upon miracle
Then when he was done, blood and water flowed

Millions of people are hurting, even dying inside, wondering why
After all what did they do to deserve the loss of themselves or
Worse yet loss of the ones they loved dearly being bystanders?

There is a lot of hurt in this world, it's endless to what causes pain
The suffering brings tears of the heart with helpless feelings, not knowing
How on earth can I ease the pains and wonder in the eyes, looking back?

There was a man that was dying but wouldn't know it by his testimony
The only other that knew was his doctor not even his family knew his fate
But he would tell anyone who listened how he turned pain to joy

Through the pain of the world led him to the Man stretched on the hill
This was where he found the love and healing he would say to the crowds
Then as He said they were loved too, blood and water flowed from his side

Those that saw this knew his testimony to be true and asked to be saved
So they too could feel the love and healing from the Man stretched on the hill
Who they now know to be Jesus Christ the Son of God

When we speak about the love and healing of Christ who died for the world
Do those that listen see the blood and water flow from your side, telling them
Your testimony is true and Christ lives in you?

Can you feel, can you see the blood and water of Christ flow from your side
No not with eyes of the flesh but eyes of the heart that's dying to be healed
Telling you the testimony you speak has been written in stone for all to see

MIDNIGHT RIDE OF THE SUN

A man stood in a tomb long ago with arms stretched rolled the stone away
Scars on His hands an side where the blood and water flowed on the cross
Now He stands at the doorway of heaven, waiting to bring us home

But until He comes blood and water flows from his side on our testimony
Sealing our words of His love and sacrifice written in the stone of His truth
So that when we tell those that are hurting by the world may believe His love

Be Still

Ever pray for someone in need of keeping a job who then lost it?
Ever pray for someone in need of healing that died in his or her sleep?
Keep praying be still and know I am God

There was a woman in jail that had just lost her family
She cried out, God doesn't exist He isn't real, then she said
God if you're real give me a sign as she fell asleep

Through a crack in the bricks a light shown through
On the floor in a dark corner the light showed two
Blades of grass that seemed to say, Be still and know I am God

Two men who were about to lose everything they had prayed upon a rock
As they were praying wind started swirling about them all around them
The wind stopped when they stopped praying, Be still and know I am God

Had a brother that was in a deep faith until one day he stumbled
Kept praying that he would regain his footing but he kept falling
wanted to give up praying when a voice said, Be still and know I am God

God is our refuge our strength an ever present help in trouble
Therefore we will not fear though the earth give way and
The mountains fall into the heart of the sea

Be still and know I am God, I hear your every prayer, your every word
I am sending the rider on the white horse, your prayers will be answered
I will be exalted among the nations, I will be exalted in the earth

Stranger In The West

There was a Stranger that would go anywhere He could on horseback
From the mountains, to the plains even across the desert He would go
On top of the mountains, underneath the sky, He would sing to heaven

If you listened to the wind you could hear the words He would be singing
Lord send me, I will go where you want me, even to the valley below
I will carry the burden, I will live through the pain

People that saw the Stranger said it looked like He was on a mission
Some even got to see the guitar hanging on the side of the saddle
They would also see the gun and wonder who He was

33 years passed by and the stories of the Stranger keep coming in, most
Would be about saving the helpless, finding the lost, bringing in outlaws
The strangest stories were about Him preaching like He was on a hill

The Stranger that shall come from a far land to help those in need
No matter what, no matter how far you are, I'm just a breath away
I will come out fighting for you until the end of days

One day an outlaw by the name of Lucifer confronted the Stranger
They had their showdown, everybody watched the Stranger die
Lucifer started walking away, when the Stranger sat up

Stranger In The West Returns

There was a Stranger that came 2,000 years ago now forgotten
His legendary stories of miracles, now seem like ten cent novels
But rest assured this hero of the west still lives

If only we still listened to the wind instead of letting it just blow past
His voice still sings words of comfort as He prepares a places for us
Just like He promised as He rode up into the clouds

The Stranger didn't stay in the west, He wasn't bound by land or sea
Not even time itself could hold the Stranger as He moves the clock
He rides in every country, speaking every language His gospel

If only we'd not limit His hands from reaching, feet from walking
After all we're the Stranger's body that's to move on His command
But if His body won't move He will find away

The Stranger will reach every soul showing how much He loves them
Even if it means crying out through Rocks in strange lands with no roads
The shame will stain those that reject His Spirit

Legendary stories will be heard like screaming wind in a cloudless sky
Yet still rains in sight of His rainbow, making the Stranger known to all
That He's Alive not only in the west, but in the east, north and south

The Stranger's name will be known to all upon His return
Everyone will know He's the truth, the way, the life above all
As He's the only Son of God, His name is Jesus Christ

What Or Who

There will be days I grow weary of dealing with the same old pain
But that's okay Lord's mercy will be waiting to give me pain relief
Just never know what or who they will be God's wonders are endless

We haven't been perfect since the bite of forbidden fruit, He knows
That's why God sent His only Son to take our imperfections to die
So that we may be perfect once again through His mercy, Jesus

There will be days I feel lost, feeling like my same old self again
But that's okay Lord's grace will be waiting to remind us He forgives
Just never know what or who will be used to be God's endless wonders

We don't have to worry about being perfect since the day we accepted
Jesus Christ into our hearts gave us His Spirit to be perfect on our behalf
Just have to give our best effort and leave the rest up to the Lord

There will be days I feel my strength drained, feel nothing in weakness
But that's okay the Lord will be my strength, my shield, He will carry me
Just never know what or who He will use to provide in our humble state

We can go to the Lord's mountain to take rest renew our strength
The Lord doesn't expect us to go through the valley alone till the end
His angels come in many shapes and forms to help us fly like eagles

Isaiah 40:31

Calling All Sinners

Calling all sinners to repent before it's too late
Not to be feared but to be set free before we can't
A day is coming when our confession won't be heard

Every knee will bow to confess Jesus is the Lord of all
And will all see the signs of His love that was the truth
That everything that came to be was because He loved

Sinners listen to the Voice that's calling us to repentance now
Before we're being called to be judge before the throne of God
Confess before a risen Savior so judgment will be passed to Him

Everything that was denied by us will come to pass as truth
Truth could've set us free, if only believed instead of trash it
Now only thing separating us from hell is one last breath

We're not being called to play politics no time to be Pharisees
Separation between church and state is passed if we want to live
Only one dictating our future rights is Jesus Christ

Everyone will be looking as Jesus comes through the clouds
Those that repented in love will go to heaven, those that refused
Will have looks if they adjust their pants as sin still stains their hearts

Calling all sinners to repent, even that which we don't call to be sin
Not to be feared of being different, so lies won't twist our fate
Give Christ our sin to be glad we did, deny and wish you did repent

Everyone sins the only difference is those that listen to His voice
They that humble before the Lord confessing the need for a Savior
Well hallelujah Jesus is my Lord that saved me from my last breath

Faith Microscope

How many of us take the time to think about things unseen?
Let alone believe what our naked eyes can never see unless
We take the time to look under a microscope

Many living things we can't see with eyes like molecules unless sneezed
Our body so complex we can't even see the cells living underneath blood
This should be proof enough that we can only be created by God

Just because we can't see something or someone, makes them nonexistent
Like the tick we failed to see till it was too late, now Lyme disease has started
If only a doctor will recognize the parasite from the drop of our blood

How many of us take the time to think about consequences of sin?
Even from a little white lie, sin takes hold like little ticks with disease
Darkness takes root deep in the soul hardening hearts to sin more

Truth told is always better, even when it hurts, the lies hurt more
Ten Commandments isn't the only sins in the Bible to be committed
Got to keep reading, keep listening to what Jesus says till obedience

Faith is God's microscope given for us to see His work, feel His presence
Through Christ alone will we get the cure, His blood to heal us from sin
The confession of needing Him, our repentance drinks His forgiveness

Jesus wants us to use the faith given while trusting in Him
Even through the storms He sends us in to strengthen faith
This is so we can have wider vision, an understanding of love

Been

Have you been stuck, dealt with addictions? Well so have I
Living at home all my life, not knowing any other options
Physical limitations gave birth to mental expectations

Dreams came and went as they died one by one
Just as another winter ends, melting with the spring
Eventually sleep came with a drought of dreams

Have you been heartbroken, dealt with rejections? Well so have I
After all, who would want to go out with a broken down? Still at home
So my mind thought until I let it all go

All of these addictions, broken hearts, scattered emotions
Gave birth to poem after poem, conceived from imagination
The daydreams while music played on all the car trips

Not all of us are born to be a chatter box, a know it all
Or with a body that works perfectly to do everything
The Lord gives us the perfect gift to watch and learn

Have you been lifted up, prayed for, blessed with friendships?
After all, God knows exactly who to put in our lives to mold us
I know He has with me, after all it's not by accident that we met

A Way Out

We may forget about the devil but he never forgets us
He knows our weakness and will tempt us with desires
Big or small doesn't matter an avalanche is waiting to fall

When one door closes, another one opens
If not always a window for us to go through
There will always be a way out

God doesn't tempt us nor can He be tempted
But will provide us with the way out if we listen
Even if we fail and fall in deeper than we can swim

Whatever the addiction, whatever the worst we've done
Don't need to give up, even when everything looks lost
There will always be Jesus to call on to get us out

Hearts are full of selfish desires that will deceive with temptation
Why we need to dig deep into the living word of God, draw closer
With Jesus it is written that the devil will flee

When a door opens that shouldn't be walked through
Look for the door or window the Lord will provide to flee
Even when we don't listen the first time, won't leave us alone

Children Need

Whatever happened to the Parents, Moms and Dads that read to children?
Let's turn off the smart devices, no screens for distraction in dreams tonight
Get back to hearing how Jesus loves the little children before we sleep

We wonder about the violence going on in the streets, of neighborhoods
While introducing our children to violent video games, on the TV screens
Instead of reading to them, introducing the love of Jesus

Whatever happened to Parents, Moms and Dads praying with their children?
Teaching them how to pray early and often will help them to listen for His voice
So they know who they can turn to, when feeling down, or peer pressure

Gun control isn't the answer when we stopped taking the Bible off the shelf
Bad enough we kicked Him out of school, but He needs to be heard at home
This means the Parents, Mom and Dad need to set the example

Children need to hear how Jesus loves them through words we speak
Children need to see how Jesus walks, by the way we walk beside Him
Children need to see Him, hear Him often while still young

Don't wait until the children grow and can be taught by someone else
Then it might be too late to hear of God's truth of how He made them
They don't need to be confused on Whose they are, they're God's Children

Storms Of No Remorse

Preparing our children for the storms to come starts at home
They're hard enough to overcome when unprepared grown up
We need to teach them what we've already gone through

Don't we know by now, storms have no remorse when it comes to age?
So why should we wait until right age of understanding what's coming?
Nobody fully grown gets it, unless shown by those that made it through

Calm before the storm is now, use the time wisely before the clouds form
Show the children by example, how to prepare for what's to come by day
So they can feel at rest by night with the prayer of devotion to give thanks

Heaven forbid, what if the storm comes and goes, leaving them alone?
Who will be left to teach the children it's okay if the storm takes us away?
That mourning isn't the end, but the beginning of our healing?

How are the children to know there are two kinds of storms in life?
That we don't have to be afraid, will never be alone in any storm?
Jesus will be with us when we're sent in, or on the way out?

Preparing our children starts with tucking them in at night with a prayer
So they know who Jesus is in their dreams as He shows them, His promise
That the Son will always come up at the break of dawn no matter the storm

Believe His Love

Defining life by the logic of our minds gets too complexing
Even though it's not that hard to comprehend the truth given
Just have to learn not everything needs to be explained

God created everything in six days, saving His most loved last
Male and Female with free will to use with a mind all our own
Even though He knew our hearts would be deceived by sin

Understanding to believe, this is how world's logic thinks
That something so simple as love could be the answers
Not understanding how faith truly works with grace

God is love, wasn't going to give up on us in a million years
No matter if it took us a million chances to finally accept Him
Thankfully He took our sins, our penalty of death in His hands

Two thousand years has gone by, but His sacrifice stands forever
Time stands still when it comes to Jesus forgiving us on the cross
His resurrection lives on through His love given to us

God knows we won't understand everything to get past our shame
That is why it takes faith to see Jesus is the living grace and truth
Just wants us to trust Him, love Him freely

Defining life by the way we love doesn't take rocket science
Believing in love will show us how the power of love is Jesus
Just got to reach out in compassion, believe His love is trusted

Loved

Wake up, get ready for school, we learn half-heartedly, then come home
With distractions of gossip, bullying in between, on screens till bedtime
Losing sight of the real purpose of educating our lives passing through

Things we do to prepare for life after school, to make success pay off
If only God's word was the textbook used, we'd know it's not money
But learning to love those around us even when they don't love us

Wake up, get ready for jobs we do half-heartedly, then come home
With distractions of gossip in between and on screens till bedtime
Losing sight of the real purpose of our lives passing through

Things we do for work is only part of our jobs to make a living
Not to make our environment an easier way to live happily after
But to make those that work around us better

Education, building ourselves up is only part of living down here
The real purpose is walking with God our Father as others watch
How we help build His Kingdom with the way we love

Those we work with, go to school with, will make those around loved
Everyone should have a shoulder to lean on as we're passing through
Until Jesus comes back, let us build His kingdom together

Learn to love with the friendships, even through betrayal
Teach to love with coworkers, even through different opinions
This might be the only love they will ever know, to know Him

Power Of The Mind

We want to strive forward till we reach our dreams
Yet something always holds us back from achieving
Our wishful thinking is stuck in a paralyzed body

Legs walk when our mind tells the legs to move
Speak when our mind tells the mouth to speak
Fear in the mind will be the backs breaking

Dreams are ours to break, depending on what we think
Negativity will be the chain that holds us like prisoners
Only our minds can keep us, only our minds can free us

We need to take control of our minds before someone else does
Satan is dying to get in at any cost, looking for every window of sin
Because he knows if he controls the mind, he controls us

Power of the mind will take us to the top or leave us six feet under
Respect the mind, careful of what the mind sees through our eyes
Reign in the tongue before it fools the mind in wrong thinking

Hearts and minds let us surrender them to Jesus Christ
Only way to free us from the chains of fear, which hold us
With Jesus, satan will be locked out, our minds will be clear

We want to strive forward till we reach past our dreams
Visions of achieving will be the reality that pushes us through
Our confident thinking faith will have us celebrating success

Out Of The Way

The only one keeping me from succeeding is myself
No matter the circumstance that comes along it's me
The temptation doesn't matter when it's my decision

Eve could have said no to satan, but she said yes
Adam could have said no to Eve, but he said yes
Nobody, nothing caused them to sin or keep sinning

So why do I keep getting in the way of myself to succeed?
How deep do I look within to find the truth I've been denying?
What am I afraid to let go of, which holds me back?

Forgiveness is bigger then the pride that keeps the hurt
Bitterness will never let go, until we let go of the madness
Need to forgive those that don't understand like Christ did

So why do I keep on denying answers beyond understanding?
The time to search has ended, must accept the truth to move
Only way forward is through trusting He who saved me

Forgiveness of myself is bigger than the hurt, the guilt kept
Got to just let go, even in the hidden secret places of our hearts
Jesus knows and He is bringing it out for us to let go

The only one keeping me or you from succeeding is us alone
Nothing in this world can keep us from reaching our full potential
When we get out of our own way, to let Jesus have control

Midst Of The Storm

Don't we know by now He sees the storm that's coming
Weather it's coming down as rain, or snow, or situations
Also should know by now we're not alone

Everything will be okay, everyone will be alright in the hands of Christ
He will hold our hands, till He guides through, until the skies clear again
Jesus won't let go until the rainbow appears

Don't we know by now, we don't have to fear the storm that's coming
Will never be left alone, not for a minute, not for one second of our lives
His promises have yet to be broken and never will

Be still and know God is holding us, loving us in His holy arms
His voice sings sweet lullabies till His peace fills our troubled hearts
He will wipe every single one of our tears away

Don't we know by now we're His forever the moment we let Him in
Jesus will never ever let us go, no matter how much we push away
His blood flows in us and will never ever run dry

Jesus stands in the midst of our ship, our body speaking to the storm
Feel the calmness return, the seas of our hardship return to still waters
The sun has come out with blue skies just as He promised

Angels And Demons

All is quiet on the outside as I sit, looking around
While my soundproofed mind is holding a war of words, match
Between angels and demons, thoughts are going out of control

Even though I write poetry for the Lord, for hope to see the light
But could just as easily be poetry for the fear seen in the darkness
Thanks to the Lord's grace that saved me, faith had been strong

We're only as strong, long as the armor of the Lord is ready for battle
Without this armor we're too weak to fend off an attack thoughts within
Won't be long till thoughts turn to actions bad or good, doesn't matter intent

Well somewhere back down the road armor fell off, felt loss of life
With nowhere to turn, heard thoughts of betrayal, felt left behind
Even though my heart and angels in my mind said differently

I wonder if this is what King David felt even though he was a king
But a king on the run as his supposed to be kingdom after him
Bet he had thoughts even though his promised throne would come

Praised be the Lord for creating us a clean heart from His blood
Even after being betrayed by us, forsaken by the Father, He forgave
Just like He planned after we first lost our armor and first sinned

All is quiet on the outside as I sit, looking around, watching
While my soundproofed mind is holding a war of words between
The angels and demons, until I put the helmet of God on

Eph 6:10-20

Impacted

Not everyone was born to impact millions of people
Some of us were born to impact the few that will
Even the ministers need ministered too

What would have happened to Billy Graham's preaching
If he wouldn't have come across the one that impacted him?
Sure maybe someone else would have come along, or not

Everyone has an important role in building the Kingdom of God
Everyone is created special, there is not one accident among us
Each of us has a need of someone to impact us in God's way

We could be doing something simple as playing cards
Next thing we know, talking to someone's daughter to save
Impact can now be seen in two lovely daughters of her own

If no one has impacted us to the point of greatness
Only means they're still coming, so keep waiting, watching
If get left behind, let them go, only means they're not the one

God didn't create us to go through life's purpose alone
He will send us brothers, sisters to guide us, impact us
We will know them by their love, light of Jesus

Mountain Mover

In my dreams I could do anything, move anything I wanted
Yet when awakened from the dream, became the weakest
Thought no way could I move that which kept me reaching

I look so tiny, feel so helpless next to this Mountain Lord
Yet you tell me to place my hands on the Mountain to move
Even with the world watching I place my hands upon because

I will be your hands, you will supply the power for me to move
Long as I leave the If, the doubt behind, faith will be unstoppable
Action of my faith will move the highest mountain

Many times we worry about the world's thoughts and doubt of us
Before we know it let the world define who we are, who to become
The world tells us being humble is for the weak

The Lord tells us being humble is our way to use His strength
Through our willingness to surrender to His thoughts, His ways
Even though seen as weak, He will be seen as strong

In my dreams reality met with the vision God had for me
Nothing upon waking up could get in the way of the Mover
Just long as I had the faith to follow

Mountain Mover you be my hands, I will supply the power
Don't be fooled, that's not your hands trembling on the mountain
That's the mountain moving under the powerful hands of God

Miracle Journey

Nobody wants to go through sickness until we become weak
The prayers of healing will come expecting a miracle to happen
The very moment Amen has been said

What if the Miracle isn't in the now of the prayer being said
But what if the miracle is in the journey of getting to the end
When we're broken and weak His glory is seen strong

Think Lazarus wanted Jesus to wait four days till raised
But no he had to go through the journey of dying to live
Wasn't until he completed being broken till he was healed

Nobody wants to go through pain, until we become weak
The prayers of healing will come expecting to suffer no more
Expecting God to heal us in our time, not His

What if the Miracle isn't in the Amen of the prayer being said
But what if the miracle is in the journey of finding His comfort
When we're seen with our eyes looking up, His glory is seen

Who would the miracle come from if nobody was willing
God needed someone to wake up too see they was dying
And that someone was me, Then He saved me

Through the valley shadow of death I came through
Fear was nipping at my heels, till Jesus took my hand
He led me through the miracle journey

Believe In You

How much longer must we follow the same footsteps?
Until we see the footsteps we follow are going in circles
We weren't born to follow the many, but the few

Twelve went into the promise land to scout as told
Only two came back unafraid of the giants in the land
But because of listening to the afraid took another 40

Logic won't always give the correct answer we seek
Sometimes we must go against logic and go by faith
Things aren't always what they seem to human eyes

Valley of the shadow of death is the way we must go
Don't be afraid, Jesus already took death to the grave
And He marches us into victory if we'd only follow Him

How much longer must we follow those like lemmings to sea?
They lost their way long time ago we're just to blind to see
The time to separate is now, before they lead over the edge

The Lord didn't create us to be like others before us
He created us before birth to be one of a kind perfectly
So have Faith to be ourselves, Believe in you like He does

Breath Of God

Jesus is the breath of God, who created everything
Nothing happens by accident, but like clockwork
Even us humans He calls His Children

God made everything with a quality to take care of themselves
Nothing in Nature happens by accident, but it's a given for every
Living creature to adapt prepared for anything that comes

Ants depend on each other to work together in order to survive
Big or small we have purpose, lessons to share for us all to learn
Even eagles need to learn to fly before flying above the storm

God holds us above everything else because He made us special
We're the only Creation made with free will to choose for ourselves
Because God wanted something to love that would love Him back

Except we chose to use free will to cost us dearly always wanting more
Instead of being satisfied with loving God the purpose of our Creation
We let satan talk us into wanting to be like God losing our way in sin

Jesus is the Breath of God who was born from a virgin named Mary
So He could walk with us, talk with us, teach us how to Love again
He did so by dying on the Cross saving us from our Sins of free will

Breath of God returned preparing for our homecoming like it first began
But those that choose to breath in deep, Jesus flows in the hearts of life
His Love was given for us to exhale freely through our will

Friends No Accident

We're not born where we are by accident but by plan
Everything God does has specific purpose, specific time
Including those He has us grow up with

Little things maybe meaningless until nurtured
Like those we hung out with as kids, growing
The things we would, or wouldn't get into

Who we're born with is no accident, but planned
God gave parents instructions to raise us in His love
So that when we heard His voice, we'd answer

Friends God put in our paths will help us grow character
Including those we think have betrayed us like Judas's kiss
Only with forgiveness our relationships grow stronger

Whether we marry or stay single is no accident, but planned
Everything God does for a man between a woman is specific
So that there's no mistake teaching our children about His love

Shame on us, shame on them if we never felt Gods love
But, rest assured God has planned for us a way to feel Him
From heaven to Earth He came born to save us and He did

We're who we are grown up as He planned no regrets needed
Everything God has done was for us to be prepared to face now
Not always for us to do something, but here to be with friends

Beauty Of The Lord

There is no way all of this beautiful creation formed from accident
We get reminded every Sunup, every Sunset that there's a God
And He loves us so much He created us to enjoy it with Him

Beauty of the Lord comes in all shapes and forms to behold
Even if we can't see it on the outside, we should know it inside
When the Lord tells us every second, with ever breath we're His

From the mountaintops to the ocean floor God made it all beautiful
With purpose for every Creature living in or under for His glory to see
They praise Him with every breath giving thanks

Beauty of the Lord can be seen in all of His Creation that's full of awe
Even in our silence praise can be felt, can be heard from our heart to His
When we have His glory living in us, can't help express Love back

Have

Have you ever looked in a mirror only to turn away
Too ashamed to look at your own face, loss of worth?
Well I have and I didn't like it so I changed

Trying to be pleasing to those I loved, but failing miserably
Nothing I did seemed good enough not understanding physically
Why my body wouldn't work, but unable to explain excuses

Have you ever fed your stress not just to satisfy hunger
Because of physical limitations unable to take it out physically?
Well I have and I didn't like it so I changed

Faith was what kept me going, Faith wouldn't let me quit
Because I knew there was something more than my world
Had to let the walls down, come out from hiding

Have you ever felt the courage come back, remember the moment
When you took shame by the throat and said no more living like this?
Well I have and I liked the change that was coming over

Feels so amazing when someone believes in you
The words 'I am proud of you' bring new emotions
Bringing the confidence back which was lost in doubt

Have the faith to keep going, even when in self-doubt
Don't be so people pleasing, some don't understand
God is watching and loves us just the way we are

One day soon two dogs will run off for you to find change
Before you know it prayers are answered under your nose
Never know until we want to change our world

Hunger Pains

Before we take our next bite, do we know what's in it?
Why are we eating? What are we eating? What's the cost?
If it's not doing the body good where does it go?

We question gun laws, drug laws, post speed limits
But do we ever question food and drink laws that kill
Or do we find it's okay to die slow and not fast

Before we take our next sip, do we know what's in it
Why are we drinking? What are we drinking? Is it worth
The bodies rejection and then where will it go?

Addictions taste good making it harder to give up
Sugar rush makes the food and soda company's rich
All the while diet Vultures are waiting for us to get fat

Wonder what would happen if we questioned everything
After all it's our bodies, making it our right to read ingredients
Not everything labeled is what it seems or agrees with stomachs

What goes into our bodies doesn't always come out
The body keeps what it likes, stores what it can't use
It's only the waste that comes out not the fat

Before we drink our next soda, next coffee what's the cost?
Before our next junk food binge what will be the final cost?
Will the diabetes, the heart attack be worth the short satisfaction

No pill can satisfy hunger pains only good nutrition
There is no substitute for what God created us to eat
Spend now for fresh save on extra years of our life later

Hoarders Of Sugar

High fructose, modified starch, just to name a few artificial
Leaves our stomachs confused, doesn't recognize its nutrition
So then why do we put it in our bodies to be stored as fat?

Hoarders keep collecting things so they say until avalanche
Strangers look on, wonder what we see in the junk we collect
Well this is the same way our bacteria feels about junk food

We're born in the natural made to eat all natural foods
But somewhere down the line we decide to eat pretty
Just like we dress, forgetting what we saw in the mirror

Hoarders of sugars from years of food addictions eating blind
Our stomachs need to make space, can't use it as nutrition
Only thing left to do is store it as fat

We can't wait for the FDA to make changes we know better
Wake up we're all capable of making smart decisions ourselves
Don't have to eat it, drink it just because someone sells it

3 Day refresh will kick addictions to the curb taken out with garbage
Our stomachs will be feeling so good finally being satisfied nutritionally
Our arteries will be singing hallelujah being able to breathe again

Hold Him

Only the One True God would allow Himself to be seen this way
No other god would dare to stoop down this humbling way of love
But Jesus just had to have relationships with you and me

He holds us three hundred-sixty five days a year twenty-four seven
Yet one Christmas morning He allowed us to hold Him or at least
We could have if we were one of the wise men or shepherds

We may not always feel Him or too blind to see Jesus holding us
But His promise of never leaving or forsaking us is forever in love
No matter how far we run or how deep a hole we fall into He's there

How many times must we hear the story of how God was one of us
That He took off His crown, came off His thrown to be born among us?
Well I hope to hear it at least until He comes back and tells me Himself

Santa Clause can have his presents, put up those trees
While I get to hold my Savior the greatest gift ever given
I don't want the whole world just want to satisfy my soul

Hand Me Down Sin

Ever since we've been birthed from our Mother's womb we sinned
We need to get this truth of being born a sinner inside our head
No sprinkle of water on Babies heads will wash this sin away

Child's lack of understanding will only save them for so long
Grow up quickly into child's faith they must, to see night light
Before the bulb burns out leaving them blind in the dark

The First Grandparents Adam and Eve's sin didn't stop with them
Certainly didn't stop with Cain and Abel's sin, just keeps coming
As if passing along the same old hand-me-down clothes

All babies will grow up to start walking, talking, thinking own thoughts
Child's innocence will only get so far, before the devil comes knocking
If only they knew not to open up to strangers inside their heads

The Heavenly Father gave us His love letter, not just to know Him
But so we could prepare for the warnings He gave us about satan
If only we'd forget our ignorance, read His book, then listen

Hand me down sin we're born into, until born again in Jesus
We need to sit in His lap as children to learn how He loves us
Our children are protected in His lap with His blood forgiveness

Ever since we've been birthed from our Savior's grace we're favored
We need to get this truth of being born of His blood inside our head
Now the sprinkle of water will mean something for claiming to be His

God's Tow Truck

The hard times aren't always about what we're going through
Sometimes it's about those living in harder times behind us
God needs someone to show what to do, to get through

The world is in darkness because of the selfishness of sin
Not everything is about what we want and what we can't have
Would have thought we'd learn from Adam and Eve by now

The pain from brokenness isn't always about us needing fixed
Sometimes reminders are needed, that pain brings on healing
Not just to us, but those needing to go through the healing next

Eating from the forbidden fruit is what made us sick to death
Yet the selfishness of sin still has us eating even with a bellyache
Thanks to the selfless act of God's love we're given a cure in Jesus

The roads we travel are broken from so many traveling the same way
With travelers broken down along the side of the road waiting for help
If only we would slow down enough to be the Samaritan they need

God uses hard times, the pains we go through to slow us down
This helps us see beyond the selfishness of our sin and repent
So He can uses us to be His tow truck in helping others get home

Grace Calling

Loss of life of those we loved can take us down a journey unknown
Much as we try preparing for the storms that might come unexpected
Somehow always end up forgetting, regretting what we left behind

Easy for us to lose our way with our heads down, eyes won't see
Not when our hearts are frozen to the point of not feeling anything
Will thaw out with the warmth of love which will help us hear

If we look up long enough will hear Grace calling, saying come back
I know it feels like the sky is falling, the world is crashing down, but
Jesus still has His arms stretched, holding your world in His hands

Times of moving, that brings on change that makes letting go hard
Even to the point of needing to pry our fingers to letting them go
No need to feel regrets, they know, they understand, they love you

Truth will always be there to set us free when we stop resisting Him
When we're free will see grace waiting to take us where love is felt
That is when will begin to feel the tingling of love mending the heart

Grace will keep calling until we listen to the Voice of Truth saying
Everything will be okay, you're losing nothing, only gaining victory
I am Grace and Truth, but you may call me Jesus, anytime for anything

Last Time

Watching TV we see what the media chooses to show what news we see
Usually the bad news comes first, tragedies come next, but what can we do
As the world try's to figure out why the outcome, why someone would do this

Everyone is looking for solutions without understanding the problem
Quick to blame false pretenses, things without a heart to love, to change
Easy to demand change, except when it's us needing to change

Pray for your enemies is what Christ Jesus said, but yet we don't
Criticize is what we do to what or who we don't like or agree with
All because of the little we see through media's eyes and ears

What gives us the right to judge on gossip from another's lips?
Everyone has the right, ability to change when love is welcomed
But the shame is on us, when we refuse to let love come through

How can we remove specs of dirt from our brother's eye being blind
When we refuse to deal with sin in our own eyes? We all need His grace
Removing sin with sin is impossible

When was the last time we prayed for those needing Jesus
Instead of crucifying them on Facebook or Twitter with jokes?
Don't need any more white lies, too many die because of them

Let us pray for those we see, even those we disagree with
Because the only way for the nations to change is revival
Coming together in repentance, so we receive forgiveness

Love Above

Wonder what would happen if we turned off our worldview
And looked through each other's eyes, felt each other's pain
Would we feel, understand each other's need of compassion?

If only we'd lay down our arms get in a room shut the door
And not come out until we said nice things about each other
Just maybe we could forgive and make up

Cain killed Abel over envy, jealousy, hurt feelings far too long
Giving into bitterness, hate never ends in satisfaction, just recycles
Only way to get off the circle of revenge is to forgive

Wonder what would happen if we looked to the heart first
Instead of looking at the shirt we wear before we think opinion
Just maybe we should stop being ashamed of our nakedness

Love God, love your neighbor is the greatest commandments
This is what Jesus said, Who came to save us, not condemn us
We're loved above all else, Jesus wants us to love above all else

Wonder what would happen if 'I am sorry' became words of strength
The only weakness is refusing to forgive the human mistakes committed
If God can forgive our endless sin, why can't we forgive their one?

All will stumble, All will fall down over tangled feet at some point
If only we would accept the hand to help us back up in forgiveness
Instead of slapping the hand away when we're just as guilty, but forgiven

Loved

Wake up, get ready for school, we learn half-heartedly then come home
With distractions of gossip, bullying in between, on screens till bedtime
Losing sight of the real purpose of educating our lives passing through

Things we do to prepare for life after school to make success pay off
If only God's word was the textbook used, we'd know it's not money
But learning to love those around us even when they don't love us

Wake up, get ready for jobs we do half-heartedly then come home
With distractions of gossip in between and on screens till bedtime
Losing sight of the real purpose of our lives passing through

Things we do for work is only part of our jobs to make a living
Not to make our environment an easier way to live happily after
But to make those that work around us better

Education, building ourselves up is only part of living down here
The real purpose is walking with God our Father as others watch
How we help build His Kingdom with the way we love

Those we work with, go to school with will make those around loved
Every one should have a shoulder to lean on as we're passing through
Until Jesus comes back, let us build His kingdom together

Learn to love with the friendships even through betrayal
Teach to love with co-workers even through different opinions
This might be the only love they will ever know to know Him

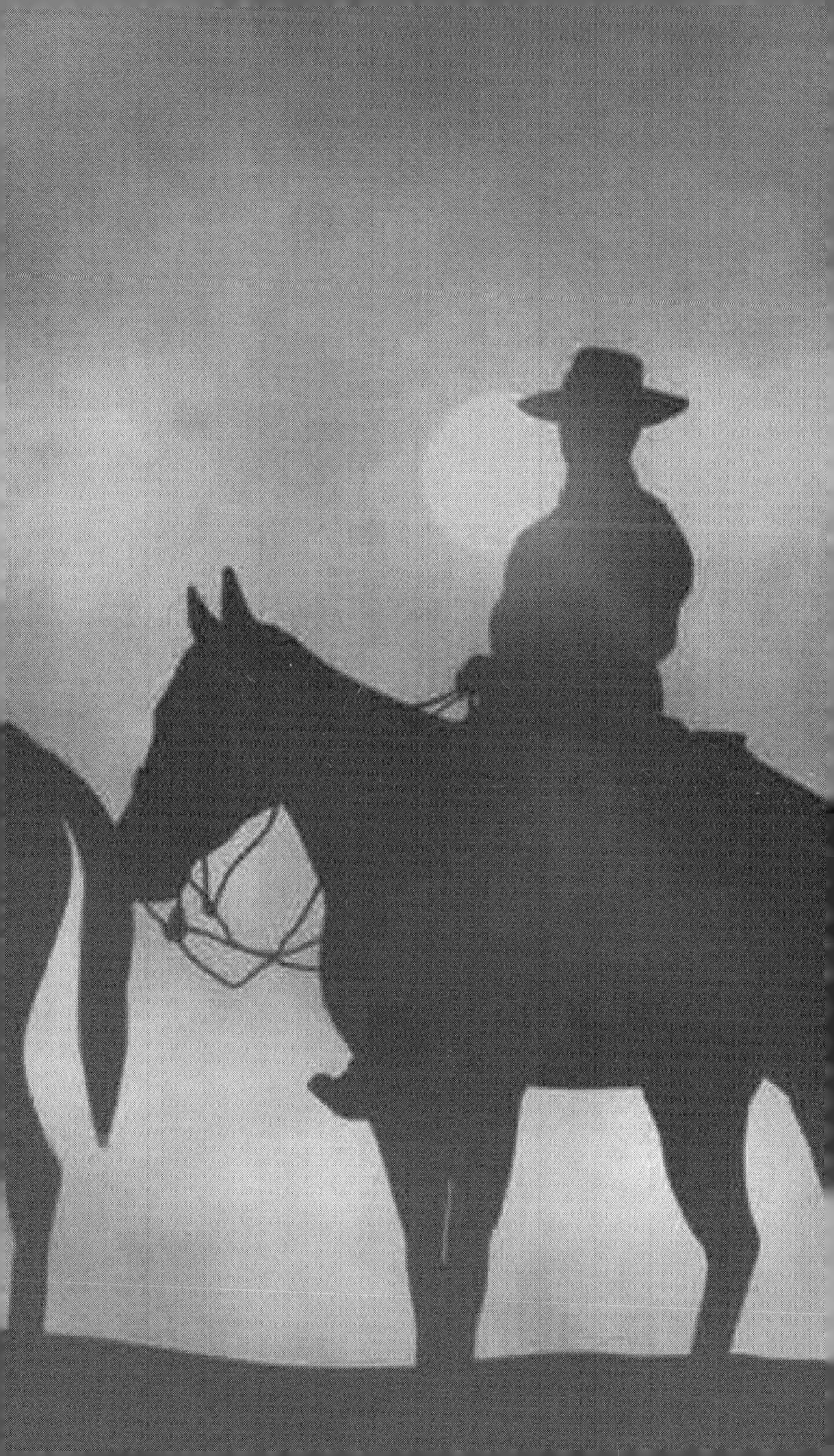

Never Know

I may never know who'll read the words I write in poetry
I may never be among the bestsellers, but that's okay
I write for the Lord and He knows who it's for

Started off as the Unknown Poet as my pen name
Not wanting to change who God made me to be
Didn't want greed or fame to take away my humility

I may never know who'll pick up my books to read
I may never sell a million, but that's okay one will do
I write for the Lord and He knows who will be touched

Started off trying to write song lyrics, until I heard nice poem
Then songs of poetry was born, just kept growing in style
All written inside my own little world

I may never know who'll be blessed until I see the face
That is reward enough for me, that is worth writing for
Thanks to the Lord for using me to make their day

Who knows? One day when I am gone, my book will be read
By someone that was lost, hurting, and it led them to Jesus
This is why I write for the Lord because He knows

No Shame In Weakness

Sickness will come and go just not always fast as we'd like
We will ask the questions of why through sickness but it's ok
Jesus is our healer, redeemer, but also friend and counselor

Shame is from the devil no need inviting either inside
Rebuke them in Jesus name because He took our shame
We need to keep our heads up, keep looking up

The answers to why we get so sick may never come from earth
But that's okay we don't need them to be healed, just faith in Jesus
When we're feeling down it means He's up to something

When we're weak Jesus will be strong in us, through us for us
No shame in weakness, no shame in being weak, for He is strong
Greater is He in us than He that is in the world

Nothing Else Matters

When we remove the sun and the moon only darkness remains
Unless we shine the light Jesus Christ gave us, which is His love
The only way to overcome the darkness is by love

Nothing else matters if we remove love
Everything else matters when we add love
Jesus just wants us to love one another

When we refuse to love, darkness of hate spreads like weeds
The more we turn away from love, will feel the hate grow instead
The hate will never stop, hate only make it burn hotter

Only thing matters is the way we love one another
No other way will do to bring everyone back together
Loving like Jesus will lead us to forgiveness

Not talking about the love from the world which fades away
But the way Jesus showed us how to love even those different
This is how we'll heal the broken and confused

Nothing else matters unless we love them first
Everyone matters when love leads faith to hope
Faith, hope, and love, greatest of these is love

Out Of The Way

The only one keeping me from succeeding is myself
No matter the circumstance that comes along it's me
The temptation doesn't matter when it's my decision

Eve could have said no to satan, but she said yes
Adam could have said no to Eve, but he said yes
Nobody, nothing caused them to sin or keep sinning

So why do I keep getting in the way of myself to succeed?
How deep do I look within to find the truth I've been denying?
What am I afraid to let go of which holds me back?

Forgiveness is bigger than the pride that keeps the hurt
Bitterness will never let go, until we let go of the madness
Need to forgive those that don't understand like Christ did

So why do I keep on denying answers beyond understanding?
The time to search has ended, must accept the truth to move
Only way forward is through trusting He who saved me

Forgiveness of myself is bigger than the hurt, the guilt kept
Got to just let go, even in the hidden secret place of our heart
Jesus knows and He is bringing it out for us to let go

The only one keeping me or you from succeeding is us alone
Nothing in this world can keep us from reaching our full potential
When we get out of our own way, to let Jesus have control

Perfect For Hype

What would we give up to be apart of the latest trend?
The cost is high, but is it worth it to be among the popular?
Even if it means trading our perfection for the hype

If only the popular made the right decisions and followed the One
But no, just like you, they're just following the crowd in hopes to be cool
They will be lucky if they only wander for forty years looking for a mirage

What would happen if we put down the popular trend magazines, tweets?
Open up the book that has the history of what happened to those following
The Bible is full of people that didn't ask the Leader who He follows

Jesus Christ is the one Way, Truth and the Life we need to follow
Who says we're perfect just the way we are, don't need the hype
Jesus already paid the price for us to rise above the rest

Why should we trade perfect for hype when the hype is lost?
The cost we can't pay to be wrong, not when the hype is death
No not from this earth, but total death in separation from God's love

Passing Through

Some believe the Bible is a book of fairytales, yet comes true
No matter the times, the technology, history repeats by mistakes
We make, over and over again, would think we'd learn by now

Logic will never come close to understanding God and His ways
Faith is the only way to truly see the marvelous works of our Creator
Yet we think because we give ourselves fancy titles we have final say

Separation church and state think they can keep God away
But that's like trying to keep the sun from rising up on the east
It's the same with our little thinking we can overpower God

The Lord created the universe from the breath of His words
The universe was nothing but blackness until God spoke light
No Big Bang was possible until man committed first sin

Some believe the Bible is a book of fairytales, yet here we are
Worried about global warming, worried about a world going mad
While satan grins ear-to-ear knowing his schemes are working

Logic will never come close to understanding it's God or satan
Faith in Jesus Christ is the only way, the Truth and the Life to see
That it's not the air we breathe, but the sin we keep that kills earth

The Lord is creating a new heaven and earth, I pray we're in it
Thanks to His mercy and grace He came down to take us there
Just have to repent and surrender to His love, His salvation

Some believe the Bible is a book of fairytales as they make home
While packing my bags finding survivors, passing through this journey
Until Jesus comes back and takes us home where we belong

Pray And Love

Somebody somewhere needs saving waiting for their superman
But what if I am Superman still going through clothes in the closet
Because we think it's the clothes that define who we are

We don't have to be called superheroes to make the difference
If being who we are is okay with God, then should be okay with us
Knowing Whose we are will help us take hold of the power needed

Invisible people must be shooting guns killing the innocent
Because all the guns are getting laws as if fired by themselves
Nobody thinks of what could be done to help the trigger finger

We don't need to be superheroes to get the villains saving the day
Nobody gets born to be villains, just treated till they're chased to dark
All they ever wanted, what we always want, just to be loved

Somebody, somewhere needs saving, waiting for their savior
What if I was Christian-man still on my knees? Could lift them
Because I don't need super powers, just need to pray and love

Just pray and love doing this will change saving the world
We don't have to get everyone, just need to pray and love
More we pray and love the more they see Jesus to change

Prayed

When things start getting worse instead of better what should we do
Natural wanting to fix, work things out by ourselves, pride only hinders
If only we prayed instead, so what are we waiting for let us pray

Don't we know when we pray without doubt all of heaven stop to listen
As God our Father listens to every word we say, hears every heartbeat
Waiting for the mighty name of Jesus to be said then He knows it's serious

Life can be going so good then change on a dime from bad to worse
Naturally wanting to find answers with the questions that keep coming
If only we prayed instead, so what are we waiting for? Let us pray

God our Father is watching, waiting, listening for us to call to Him
All of heaven is on alert waiting to sound the trumpets of Almighty
Help will be ours if only we'd call out to Jesus

The help we get isn't always like we expect thinking we'd get out
Sometimes He comes to help us get through the hard times in life
Wanting us to strengthen our faith so we don't depend on the natural

All of heaven have stopped to listen as we pray to God our Father
He listens to every word, every heartbeat, wipes every tear away
Waiting for the mighty name of Jesus to be said Amen

Bowing my head down to pray I hear the silence of heaven
Then can't help but smile hearing the voice of God the Father
Feels so good just to hear His voice as my heartbeats praises

Habit to Pray

One prayer at a time before we rise with the coming dawn
Not just to make sure we don't stumble getting out of bed
But to know the part we play today in doing the Lord's will

Lost in the world we become when we don't take the time to pray
Not just to the world, but lost in ourselves, that no mirror recognizes
When we pray to Jesus, And in Him only will we find our way

One step at a time we must take until we're shown the right way
No need to get ahead of the light, that leaves us blind in the dark
That's how will get lost in the world that forgets to pray in Jesus

We're all going to get ahead of the light until we stumble in darkness
Just a matter of time till our match of a light burns our fingers then dropped
Depending where we stand will have the match go out, or set a world on fire

Habits between a Believer and an Unbeliever is a step and a prayer
Instead of a prayer then a step, it pays off to know where we're going
The more we forget to pray before moving, more we lose our way

Following in Jesus's footsteps is the way to go about doing Father's will
If we don't see His footsteps, then we passed Him or He's carrying us
Either way it be wise to ask where He's going so we don't get lost again

This world needs more people making it a habit to pray and pray often
There's too many lost wandering in a darkened world from our foolish sin
Because they don't pray to Jesus whose glory shines a way out of the dark

Midst Of The Storm

Don't we know by now He sees the storm that's coming?
Whether it's coming down as rain, or snow, or situations
Also should know by now we're not alone

Everything will be okay, everyone will be alright in the hands of Christ
He will hold our hands, till He guides through, until the skies clear again
Jesus won't let go until the rainbow appears

Don't we know by now, we don't have to fear the storm that's coming?
Will never be left alone, not for a minute, not for one second of our lives
His promises have yet to be broken and never will

Be still and know God is holding us, loving us in His holy arms
His voice sings sweet lullabies till His peace fills our troubled hearts
He will wipe every single one of our tears away

Don't we know by now we're His forever the moment we let Him in?
Jesus will never ever let us go, no matter how much we push away
His blood flows in us and will never ever run dry

Jesus stands in the midst of our ship, our body speaking to the storm
Feel the calm return, the seas of our hardship return to still waters
The Sun has come out with blue skies just as He promised

Precious

Satan sends demons to claw and scratch at our souls
Trying everything to get us to give it up so he can steal
Because he knows it belongs to the Lord

The pain we feel deep within is the claws we feel scratching
Without Christ in us we're powerless to protect our precious
Only one way for us to feel free and it's to surrender to Jesus

Emptiness won't go away until we fill it with water that doesn't evaporate
Satan knows this, why he does everything in his power to tempt with anything
That will distract us from the truth about everlasting being real in Christ

Satan will keep clawing at our souls till we lose our minds, till we lose it
Trying every one of our weakness against us, until we breakdown for good
Don't we get it satan's days on earth are dying so He seeks revenge on us

Surrendering our Soul to Jesus Christ will set us free by the Price He paid
Because Jesus gave His life on the cross for us, so satan can't touch us
With Jesus living in us, there is no room for satan to claw at our Souls

Satan I rebuke you in Jesus name who I freely give my soul to
Nobody can touch or take what or who belongs to Jesus Christ
He fills my soul with His Holy Spirit so my precious feels free

Pry To Let Go

Don't know why it hurts so much to lose what I loved most
After all took so long to get, so held on tight to not let go
Now it feels if someone ripped them out of my hands

You know might not hurt as much if we learned to just let go
Because God doesn't want us to be in pain, yet knows best
That until we learn to let go, He will continue to pry our hands

Have we yet to learn about taking something that's not ours?
How our parents had to pry our hands until we let that go?
Not to make us sad, but to protect us against the unknown

Two hands are what we have to hold and carry burdens or blessings
We just can't always tell if it's the blessings or the burdens we hold
Not when we refuse to open our hands, can't be afraid to let go

If we want the pain to go away then must let go of what we're holding
If God is taking something from us it's because it's a burden not a blessing
He sees the unknown of what we hold and if it shows His true light

Don't know why it took me so long to let go of my burdens
Soon as I let go the pain stopped, as Jesus gave me blessings
He wasn't taking away, He was replacing with something better

Puzzle Pieces

Life can be so hard when struggling to find purpose
All of our dreams keep coming up nightmares in reality
We just can't give up, we all have a place to call home

I know might not seem like it now, but will fit in somewhere
Sometimes other pieces to life have to fit in before we find it
Our time is coming when it is our turn to shine the light

Sometimes we're edge pieces, other times we're middle pieces
We all have a role to play for this world to shine out of the dark
Just can't give up before we have a chance to fit where we belong

God uses each and every one of us at the right time, right reason
We may not understand it all until we see Him face-to-face in heaven
But every thing we go through has a purpose that He uses for good

Puzzle pieces scattered in the wind only one can find us in time
Jesus will put us all back together just have to let Him lead us
One by one we'll be put back together to be complete again

Life doesn't have to be so hard just keep looking up
Dreams will become real as God's plans come together
Before we know it we're finding our place even if it's last

Sometimes we're the edge piece that starts the puzzle
Other times we're the middle piece that help others fit
There will always be a final piece to complete the picture

Don't lose hope if we can't find our place just not our time
Patience will guide us, wisdom will provide when to move
When you see no pieces only means the final piece is you

Raised

A Mother ostrich came across an egg looked abandoned so adopted
She sat on the egg though not her own, but raised it when it hatched
Even though the baby bird named Spirit looked nothing like her own

How are we to grow when not even knowing who we're to become?
Not that we care when lived as children until the teen years passed
Then every friend has found their purpose except us

Being raised a bird of a different feather, yet awkward in its walk
With legs being shorter than the rest of the family that took him in
Yet everyone was jealous of Spirit's growing wingspan

What are we to do when we don't even know whose we are, let alone
Know how to make something so we're looked up to, not down upon, as if
Success is earned? How others judge us on accomplishments in riches

The Spirit was looking down at its own reflection in a puddle of water
Was startled when a flying bird came down and asked "why it was walking
When should be soaring high" Spirit was in awe as this bird looked like him

The help we need from mentors matters in how we're raised so we grow
Whether from our Fathers or best friends, but someone wiser than us
This is how we keep from wandering away from who we're made to be

Spirit was no ostrich, had no one to tell him who he really was, an eagle
Instead of running along the ground, should have been flying high above
But no one taught Spirit how to fly until His Mentor came along

Why are we running instead of flying on eagle wings like we're born to fly?
We're created in God's own image made to soar above the darkest storms
We need to be reminded every day that Jesus raised us up on His Spirit wings

Rest Assured

The Lord sees all, knows everything that comes our way
He allows sickness, physical weakness to come upon us
Rest assured He will bring us through till all is well

Sit down, put up the feet, get comfortable might be here awhile
If feeling low, free to ask for more comfort, the Lord gives plenty
Joy of the Lord will always be in us, just waiting to be left out

Job suffered, Paul suffered, all of God's chosen has suffered
Not because God wanted them to, but because satan attacks
Everyone he fears and his only hope is to turn us against God

Stand up, lift the hands up high, get comfortable praising Jesus
If feeling weak, give shouts of praise, Jesus is, Jesus is coming
The joy of the Lord will be felt as we see satan run

The Lord sees all, knows everything that comes our way
He allows blessings, miracles of many kinds for our faith
Rest assured get comfortable His Glory will be seen in you

Sick Dying Eden

Don't know why some good people get sick and die
While others live long and happy lives without a cold
Some answers on earth may never be found

Downfall of forbidden fruit, the cost of wanting more
Never being satisfied brought sin, sickness, into play
Keeping us just out of touch from what we called home

Don't know why some people can't live being content
While others live simply and peaceful lives without wanting
Some things on earth may never be found

Blame is all we seem to find in lies, instead of accepting truth
Like hanging onto a dying branch, only matter of time till it breaks
Passing by which could save us as we fall, if only we reach for Him

Don't know why some keep trying to make up for the guilt we done
While others live like they were born again given a second chance
Some lost on earth may never be found pray it won't be me

Christ dying on the cross is all that stands between returning home
Like hands reaching out trying to catch those that fall under repentance
Grab hold with confession that will send us through Salvation

I know why some Lazarus's get sick and die only to be raised again
Weakness of the flesh will be the strength of His glory being shown
Christ will rise us too then will all be reunited going home

Shadow's Darkness

Shadows can't be seen in darkness just all blends together
Need the light to bring the shadows out of hiding to be seen
If only we'd have Jesus to cast them out

No way can satan be real? He's just like the boogieman a myth
As his shadow blends in the darkness that corrupts our minds
Hiding under our bed ready to strike with our disbelief

Somehow if something or someone can't be seen, they can't exist
Just like Lyme disease hiding in our blood, yet messes with our system
How many positive signs will it take for us to believe we're not alone?

Shadows in our heart fogs up the mind into playing tricks
As sin runs deep in our veins, hatching out evil thoughts
If only we could get open heart Jesus surgery

Dr. Believer and Mr. Atheist we've become living one way
While denying the very truth right in front of our one eye closed
With sunglasses on while reading in the dark

Shadows be demons that takes over unclaimed souls to possess
That the world can't see because of the darkness that corrupts
Those in this world can't do anything, but point fingers

Jesus is the only one able to cast out the shadows in this world
He is the glory that shines, the light needed to overthrow demons
This is the same light shining through True Believers

Calling all Believers to turn on His light, time to be seen in this world
We need a revival like never before, time to send the shadows running
Jesus, we need Jesus to come out of our closest to shine His glory

Risen Death

Death could strike anyone at any moment, but don't have to fear
No matter the hand that delivers, no matter the way death happens
Long as we have Jesus living inside us death won't be the end

Terror may think it has the upper hand, but God is still in control
They don't dictate who lives or dies, time had already decided fate
Jesus had already come for those that loved Him, to fly like eagles

Good will be the final outcome, no evil will have the final say
God will use satan's evil intentions to better His glorious kingdom
Death is only a door for the faithful to get their job well done rewards

The only reason to fear death is if we have yet asked Jesus to save us
Because of Jesus dying on the cross for our sins we have been forgiven
But Jesus didn't stay dead, but has risen, defeating death's hold on us

Keep on serving the One that saves until we see Him return best we can
No need to fear with God's angels watching over us until our work is done
When we see the angels flee no worries it's only because Jesus is here

Let us pray for the hearts to lose the hate that hardens them to no remorse
We don't have to understand to mourn the loss of those we loved, just accept
Jesus saved them to use them, one last time to save us so we can be reunited

Revolution Of Repentance

Have we forgotten the history of America learned or is it no longer taught
Since the reason this country was founded, God was kicked out of schools
That the whole reason for Pilgrims coming was to worship Him freely

How long are we going to have history on repeating mistakes over again?
Living in the past future is denial of learning to move on, from lies to truth
We can either accept the rope of Jesus to get out of quicksand or die in it

This isn't the country our forefathers fought the Revolution for, instead
This country is becoming what they fought so hard against all over again
The constitution is being erased, the forefathers being put to shame

Wake up America before we become slaves again to a dictatorship rule
The freedom every American soldier died to save will be lost for nothing
All to keep the sinners of no remorse happy in their delusional reality

Freedom to believe the truth of which this country was founded on God
We're letting them take away our right to worship God publicly unashamed
Which is by living, following His truth, through our right to repent

Revolution of Repentance will save this country through acts of love
Not by force, but the melting of sinner's hearts will let Jesus fix the broken
The remorse will be felt, till the knees of repentance brings forgiveness

But until we repent we're stuck laying on our backs in quicksand
The rope of Jesus inches away, waiting for us to be saved, yet
Here we are dreaming, while drowning in a world never ours to own

Sleeping

What if Joseph and Mary came into our neighborhood today?
Would we be kind enough to invite them in or let them pass by
Without even noticing when looking down at a two inch screen?

While we were sleeping Jesus was born in a manger yet again
Because we didn't give Him a thought of leaving a door open
Yet He thought of us when leaving His throne to be like us

Thankfully while we're sleeping Jesus watches like a Shepherd
Even when ungrateful for waking us up before danger hits
His love will never fail even when we choose to blame Him

What if we're the chosen disciples taken to the garden to pray
Would we be sleeping instead of praying beside Jesus who was,
Who still is praying over us, while preparing to take up our Cross

While we're sleeping Jesus prays nonstop even when we forget
He still sweats blood while we're drooling on our pillows while dreaming
If only we'd be awake enough to receive His vision

Thankfully while we're sleeping Jesus watches like a shepherd
Even when we're sleepwalking guides us through the valley of death
So when we do wake up we're beside still waters in His garden

I am so thankful Jesus chose to knock on my door for me to let in
I made sure to make room inside my heart, and now He lives in me
Because of this I hear Him, See Him praying even when sleeping

Sons, Daughters

Dust and bones we're made from day six until Eve looked
Into the devil's mirrored eyes to see past the perfect truth
And took a bite into the forbidden lie that changed everything

Sad how we look into the same mirrored eyes that Eve looked into
Fall for the deception instead of seeing the truth that God created
Why change something so perfect as God made you?

Take a look around, up to the mountains, to the oceans below
God's beautiful creation is all around us, yet we refuse to see
That it is you and me the most beautiful, that God holds dear

Don't we know that God moved heaven and earth as Jesus
Through death's crucifixion, going through what was our hell
Until our road to salvation was complete through His resurrection

When are we going to smash the mirror that wants to change us?
We don't need changing, we need saving with the blood of Jesus
Then will see the mirror of truth that will show who we are

Sons, Daughters of the most High living God is whose we are
Who made us just the way we are to complete His perfect plan
Imperfections we see are what make us special, it's who we are

Dust and bones we're made from, so dust and bones will return
Until Jesus comes for us, to put us in bodies no mirror can reveal
Only royally felt as we take our place beside our King Of Kings

Spread The News

God's not calling us to be perfect, our mistakes are accepted
We've already been forgiven, we're just being asked to trust
That long as we love one another that He will do the rest

Christ hung out with the sinners unashamed of appearance
Wasn't worried about who saw Him dining with the rejected
He just loves us until the sin comes right out of us

God's not calling us to do the impossible, our weakness is accepted
We've already been risen up, His strength is taking over our brokenness
All we need to do is relax and enjoy the ride as His wings fly us

Christ sits us on His lap, we're all His children, age doesn't matter
Wasn't worried about being weighed down by our sin, just held us
He just wants us to feel His love because this is when we let sin go

God's not calling us to be Christ, just to love with Christ as He loves
We've been loved with open arms waiting for us to trust Him enough
This is when we feel the sin fall, as we let go to love back

Christ's love is enough for every cup to overflow like waterfalls
He doesn't want us to be a dam, but free of debris to leave no doubt
As His love transfixes our blood to be washed clean

God's calling us to come Home, wants us to spread the news
That Christ's love for the world was enough if they believed
He was the Son of God that they wouldn't kill, but be saved

Storing Nuts

Since when did we start growing big bushy tales on our busybody?
Life on this earth shouldn't be how much to save on this dying earth
But who we want to take with us when it's time to go home

Have we been trying to find places to store our nuts far too long?
Don't let striving for wealth blind us until we lose sight of the truth
When we were kicked out of Eden it was only temporary

Just because we mark our territory doesn't make it owned
What God gives, He can take away after all He created everything
Putting names to paper means nothing, not how God works

Have we forgotten where we buried our nuts again like squirrels
Only to find they grew into something never imagined in our mind?
What we thought was our dreams, now turned into nightmares

No need to stay in the trees fussing at those below, just wake up
Stop acting like squirrels, give all to Jesus in total surrender to Him
Only His blood will be recognized as a covenant to God

Storing nuts on earth isn't what we're called to do, but to reconcile
Then make disciples like Jesus said, before returning to His throne
We can't put treasures before the people we're called to witness

Walk To Talk

Let our walk be our talk, not just the signs we hold
What good does it do if we walk opposite of our truth?
Otherwise we're just dust in the wind

The world is watching, waiting to catch us in a lie
That's too thin a line for me to walk, I am no gymnast
I don't want to be called a hypocrite

Let our actions be the way of life we live, not just post
Don't let our phones define who we are, who we become
Our voices still need to be heard with our walk

The lost don't notice those going in same downstream
But will wonder why we decide to go against the current
The curious will want to follow, to know more

Let our walk be our talk online or offline Jesus still sees us
He doesn't need an IP address to find us, just our hearts
All He wants us to do is love one another like He loves us

Story In A Poem

Few people really know me, let alone what I've been living with
Keeping to myself most of the time, opening up to very few in life
Never really knew if anyone was really listening to my story

Life was all fun and games, hanging out with friends at church
While learning all about how Jesus loved the children in the Bible
Faith grew as times of age changed, when games became real

Physical changes can really slow a body down to the point of confusion
So confusing, to the point it can't be explained, so you can be believed
Stead of sounding like excuses to get out of work

Games for fun became distractions for the pain, dreams I wanted to live
More so when my physical body wouldn't let me live the life I really wanted
Thankfully music gave me peace, places to go till my head cleared

Labels given really do make, or break ones confidence to the point
Purpose can be quickly found, or becomes a life time of searching
The journey of purpose isn't easy, but gets better as we learn faith

Growing faith was my turning point, the only direction of my desperation
Giving up wasn't going to happen, God had plans for me, I wanted to see
Somehow, someway was going to make a difference, like I've always wanted

God's timing isn't our own, even when growing pains are many
The breaking only means we're not done being fixed to be used
God uses our brokenness to reach the lost, so they know it's okay

Humble silence that's just being me, will talk when spoken to, but I listen
Fame and fortune isn't what I look for, just simply want to make a difference
While writing poetry given by God as my calling

Learning to use life hurts as stepping stones or healing stones for others
Either through poetry or songs, everyone needs encouraged to keep going
We're not meant to travel through this world alone, but with Jesus our Savior

Swain Born

In every lake there is a Swan that is more majestic
But not every lake has a Carrie Swain born to lead
Or the wellness it takes to spread compassion

Outside Strength doesn't always show the true warrior inside
The heart is the biggest muscle and carries us through victory
No matter what or who comes our way

In every world there is a swan that is more majestic
But not every world has a Carrie Swain born to love
Or the wellness it takes to help others believe

Locked doors doesn't always mean someone's away
But could be too afraid at the sound of a knocked door
Until a sweet caring voice can be heard on the other side

In every house there is a swan that is more majestic
But not every home has a Carrie Swain born to welcome
Or the wellness it takes for a house to serve the Lord

Open doors lead to fulfilling hearts with Christ's love
That lives on forever thanks to caring out of their way
Because they took the time to say we go for No

Tear Glass

For everyone that cries into their pillow at night you're not alone
Because an unseen hand catches those tears and uses them
What hurts us deeply now, will be used to transform

The tide of God's love is always at work collecting our impurities
Will come and take our past mistakes, our shame, even our sin
Jesus then takes them in His hands and transforms for His glory

Walking along the shore of our hearts will find broken pieces we think
Until we look closer to find someone else's broken heart transformed
Which God will use to heal another heart even our own

What we take for granted in our hurt, we throw away not knowing
The tide of God's love collects, which gets tossed around until ready
This is when the tide comes in bringing our tossed trash made to treasure

The tide of God's love is always at work just like the ocean taking impurities
Using the moon, God's glory to reach in pulling out our brokenness to transform

Until the Son is ready to show us how we're used to His perfection
Someone, somewhere, somehow will walk along our heart's shore
They will pick up our use to be broken pieces that God left behind

This is how our brokenness will be used to transform them
For everyone that wakes up feeling the Son on their faces you know
Because the tears of sorrow tossed in the tide of love have returned
The once soaked pillow, now dry holds our tear glass made with His love

The Dawn

Dark of the night might feel all around us even during the day
But don't fret, don't lose hope Dawn will always be on the horizon
The Son will rise within reminding us once again He is there

Will be there for the Dawn, as the Dawn has been here for us
Even the Dawn needs a light to hold on until the Son is on high
Even as the sunsets He will be with the Dawn till time to rise again

Don't worry, about what tomorrow brings in the dark of night
Not even the birds worry about surviving the coldest of nights
They know when the Dawn comes God will provide food again

Will be here for the Dawn, as the Dawn has been there for us
I know the Dawn needs His light to hold, until He the Son rises
Even as the Dawn brings the rain, the Son is always light on us

Clouds may hover over us in the dead of night with no hope
Until the rain pours out of us and the Dawn dries our tears away
With the Son shining through the rainbow He's promised

The rainbow is there for the Dawn, as the Dawn is there for the rainbow
Even the Dawn has the promise given that their will always be a Son to bring
No matter how many sunsets come and go, He will be here for the Dawn

Thou With Thee

Even though my world has been shattered in a million pieces
I know thou will be with me until all the pieces are mended again
Just not the same world I knew

Thee will be with us no matter if we're walking or falling
Shaking of the fist He will understand, He's been there
Even Jesus questioned why He was forsaken by the Father

Even though the pain feels like it will never go away in this life
I know thou will be with me hand in hand until your love is felt
Just not the same love that I knew

Thee promised to take us through the shadow of death
Didn't say what shape we'd be coming out the other side
Just that will be for our good

Being left behind can feel lonely until we see His shadow light
Thou will always be with us, keep looking up to see His glory
Just will be seeing as never before seen

Thee will be there to comfort, there to love till peace be still
Even though will never be the same weak faith, only stronger
Just didn't say He'd be with us alone, but with those we loved

Truth Is Hard

Living easy has made us forget that we're not here to stay
Becoming so busy to make our living on earth even easier
So easy, that when change does come we fear it

Those that have passed before us would be shaking their heads
As we forget how they paved the way through blood and sweat
Not to make life better to live, but to survive until Jesus took them

Dream world has been our way of living, like playing house
Except our game has become reality, leaving us confused
So confused we no longer no what we are, let alone who

This isn't the country our forefathers fought so hard to free
Instead it's gone back to living before the written constitution
Except this time we lack the courage to start another Revolution

Politically correct is our way of living, so we don't hurt any feelings
Instead of telling the dream world to wake up to a coming harsh reality
That God put us here not to play house, dress up, but to serve Him

Satan has us living in his dream world of sin, distracting us from truth
Which is the resurrection of Jesus Christ after Jesus died for our sins
Defeating hell and the grave, so we don't have to lose courage

Those that have passed on stand with Jesus who tell us to take courage
That His revival is coming, we need to use this courage to stand ourselves
The King of Kings is coming on a white horse

Living for the Truth is hard, but living easy will be harder
When the tribulations begin, we haven't seen nothing yet
All the money we worked to live for won't save a dying world

Two Worlds One Bridge

There's a world that's hurt and lost that looks across to the other world
They wonder what makes them so content, as if they found everything
Makes them wish there was a way to cross over

If only there was a bridge for them to cross over, to experience
What we got to feel when we took the leap of faith, believed enough
Oh how life changed when I crossed that bridge

There's a world that's happy and found that looks across to the other world
They wonder what makes them so miserable to the point of hurting themselves
Wish they could come over to my world and experience true happiness

If only there was a bridge for them to cross over, to experience
What they have been missing all this time while saving to buy
Something that can't be bought only given by crossing the bridge

There are those stuck between worlds that think they're happy
But look like they suck on lemons and limes all their lives in lies
Thinking they found another bridge to cross only to breakaway

If only they crossed the one true and only bridge of Jesus Christ
Who died on the cross, the bridge between two worlds life, death
Heaven and hell, only way to true joy and happiness is through Him

Watchtowers

Has everyone fallen asleep in their watchtowers as the enemy approaches
Have we fallen for satan's worldly distractions as time gets closer to the horizon
Instead of using advanced technologies for gain, it's being used against

Comrades are doing their jobs given depending on us to watch their backs
Yet here we are with heads down watching life on a loop as reality happens
When we do look up will find our enemy with the upper hand

Instead of being in our watchtower, will be prisoners of our own demise
While the Comrades are being rescued for being faithful to God's word
Will be sent to the dark room in the black hole

Paul and Silas were rescued while they were singing praises
Not while they we're watching, debating the latest hot trends
Following Jesus is the only way will ever be rescued

Let us get back up to the watchtower before the thief comes in the night
Don't make the same mistake with the enemy, this time mercy won't be shown
And will be left all alone with the tribulations to come

Mathew 24:43, 2 Peter 3:10, Revelation 3:3, 16:15

Wisdom Angel

If there was anyone that cancer be scared of it's this woman
A Woman of God with no fear of death, faith to move mountains
This is my friend Wisdom with a Latino kick

When we're weak He is strong, He is faithful in all His ways
The Lord will take care of His angels that He puts on this earth
Who He sends to not only protect us, but to carry His voice

If there was anyone that satan feared more then Jesus, its this woman
A Woman of God with no fear for him, with faith to move mountains
This is my friend Wisdom with a Latino shaking finger

When we grow weary He carries us, He is faithful in all His ways
The Lord will take care of His angels that He puts on this earth
Who He sends to guide us in understanding His love

If there was anyone that over flowed with Gods love it's this woman
A Woman of God with a heart filled with love for some one like me
This is my friend Wisdom with a Latino twinkle in her eyes

When she is weak, He is strong, He will forever be faithful in His ways
The Lord will take care of this angel that He put on this earth to touch
Who He uses to draw us closer to understanding His grace

Worst

Whatever circumstances we get put through know it's not the end
Keep going forward no matter what gets in the way will get through
Because it won't be the worst thing we go through

The pain maybe deep, the loss maybe great, but everything will be okay
Sorrows will go, tears will be wiped away, the Son will come out shining
Nothing we go through will be the worst thing in the world

Long as we have Jesus Christ living in our hearts as Savior will survive
Because nothing will be worse than being separated from the love of God
The pain will be ten times worse than what will ever go through

No matter what sin will commit forgiveness will be ours for the confessing
There's nowhere we can run or hide from the love of God who died for us
That love is named Jesus Christ who took every sin with His blood

Worst thing we can do is reject the redemption for our salvation
Short of that, everything we go through will survive, will thrive forever
Nothing in this world can match the power of the love of Jesus Christ

With the death in the grave defeated this world has no sting
Sickness will come and go, disasters will happen, but will live
Not even satan's worst can overcome Jesus Christ's best

The worst is gone, the best is yet to come, but will be soon
Jesus will be coming to bring us home, sorrow will be gone
Will be healed, will be delivered and will be with those we love

Him Generously

My Grandfather is a kind and gentle soul full of humility
I could shake my fist in anger at what cancer is doing
But I choose to take this time with Him great joy

Don't let fear of death, fear of loss on this world steal from us
They have run the race, fought the good fight for the King of Kings
Their just reward is in sight in the very arms of The great I Am

My Grandfather's wisdom will live in the hearts He's touched
Could turn away in anger at what cancer has taken from me
But I choose to take this time with Him generously

Don't let selfishness steal from those we love blind of their joy
They have passed through a strange world since birth on a mission
They have family, loved ones waiting for them to come home

My Grandfather's endless same jokes will always be remembered
Not because of being told over and over, but because of the joy
Why I can't be angry when death is just a welcome mat to heaven

No need to fear what has no power over us, long as we're His
Not when Jesus will come like a thief in the night to raise us up
When old, decayed bodies will become new bodies with no pain

Don't stop running the race just because they finished before us
If we'd look around we'll see them now cheering us on every step
They're just no longer alone or in pain, just loving us with Jesus Christ

After the eagle took Grandfather home to be reunited with Grandma at last
I can see Grandpa walking with Jesus in heaven with Grandma by his side
I can hear Him telling Jesus about the three legged chicken as laughter echoes

"Three Legged Chicken"

A man was driving along a rural road one day when he saw a three-legged chicken running down the road. He was amused enough to drive along side it for a while, as he was driving he noticed the chicken was running 30 mph.

Pretty fast chicken, he thought, I wonder just how fast it can run. So he sped up and the chicken did too! They were now moving along the road at 45 mph! The man in the car sped up again, to his surprise the chicken was still running ahead of him at 60 mph!!!

Suddenly the chicken turned off the road and ran down a long driveway leading to a farmhouse. The man followed the chicken to the house and saw a man in the yard with dozens of three legged chickens. The man in the car called out to the farmer "How did you get all these three legged chickens?"

The farmer replied, "I breed 'em. Ya see it's me, my wife, and my son living here and we all like to eat the chicken leg. Since a chicken only has two legs, I started breeding this three legged variety so we could all eat our favorite piece."
"That's amazing!" said the driver "How do they taste?"
"Don't rightly know, I ain't caught one yet!"

Lost Not Gone

Where have you gone my friend? Haven't felt you since the day
My world came crashing down, found myself lost in mourning
When I came back, you were gone along with my heart

Thought I felt you once, but then like a mirage disappear again
I sure do miss you my friend, wish you would come back soon
Don't know how long I can take not hearing you in my head

Don't know what we've lost until a storm takes it away, then it's blown away
Now it's too late to think what could've we done besides taken for granted
But it's not too late to honor them through living as if they're with us, watching us

Picking up the missing pieces that never fell, is never easy to find
That's because Jesus was there catching them as they broke away
But He doesn't always fix it like it was, He makes it totally new again

Jesus isn't always walking on the waters during the storm for us to see
Sometimes He's just inside sleeping, when we lost faith and panicked
But rest assured the wind and the waves will calm when faith is trusted

Thought you were gone for good, but then I remembered your promise
Then I felt His hands putting everything made wholeheartedly with grace
Peace like a river began flowing again as you tell me what to write lovingly

He's Glory

Life isn't always about success, but how we finally reach destination
Rarely does one make the Promised Land in one leap, nobody is superman
Everyone starts at the beginning and goes through the crossroads

The world sees failures as being weak, where God sees success
Everyone that God has written about was far from being perfect
Everyone had to go through his or her flaws, failures and challenges

Not everyone that sees the successful outcome will be inspired
Not when his or her hope to be somebody is hanging off the edge
They need to see those beside them on the same cliff make it

The world's view of success is taking the glory for its own
Even though the glory isn't earned or even bought by the world
Satan knows this, yet doesn't stop trying to make us think we can

We're not born to become God's glory it's not our success to have
God created us to bask in His glory so His Love can be seen alive
Even though our sin kept us apart, it's His glory that brings us back

Unfortunately there are those still lost on the edge of giving up hope
Even though they still don't understand the emptiness inside the soul
The confusion of purpose has them up on the gallows

Life's weakness is His strength being shown through our humbleness
Imperfections of our walk is what makes His footsteps become known
God uses our struggles, mistakes for His Glory to shine through the dark

Story of our success will be remembered when we let struggles be known
This will be our Hand helping them down from the gallows restoring hope
Showing its giving God the Glory for what He did for us on the Cross

Spread The News

God's not calling us to be perfect, our mistakes are accepted
We've already been forgiven, we're just being asked to trust
That long as we love one another that He will do the rest

Christ hung out with the sinners unashamed of appearance
Wasn't worried about who saw Him dinning with the rejected
He just loves us until the sin comes right out of us

God's not calling us to do the impossible, our weakness is accepted
We've already been risen up, His strength is taking over our brokenness
All we need to do is relax and enjoy the ride as His wings fly us

Christ sits us on His lap, we're all His children, age doesn't matter
Wasn't worried about being weighed down by our sin, just held us
He just wants us to feel His love because this is when we let sin go

God's not calling us to be Christ, just to love with Christ as He loves
We've been loved with open arms waiting for us to trust Him enough
This is when we feel the sin fall, as we let go to love back

Christ's love is enough for every cup to overflow like waterfalls
He doesn't want us to be a dam, but free of debris to leave no doubt
As His Love transfixes our blood to be washed clean

God's calling us to come Home, wants us to spread the news
That Christ's love for the world was enough if they believed
He was the Son of God that they wouldn't die, but be saved

Since The Moment

Since the moment we first sinned God's been finding our way home
Though we've been broken and lost wondering endlessly in the dark
The pieces left behind He has picked up

Jesus has always been there, waiting for us to remember Him in paradise
Clues were left for us to find, but we kept tripping over them moving on
All the while we kept sinning, leaving more brokenness behind

Since the moment of God's first creative breath He had us in mind
No coincidence we're created last as He loved us with all His breath
Everything we've needed was waiting for us to be born

Jesus has always been there from the beginning, of first creation
Clues were in front of our faces, but darkness of sin blinded us
And we never realized it was His breath, not ours guiding us home

Since the moment of God giving us free will even though He knew
God knew when and where we'd first sin, but allowed us to learn
Why He was planning our rescue from the start of time

Jesus has been, always will be the Breath of God that gives us life
Clues were in front of our shouting faces as God's breath stopped
For two whole days creation was without breath as our sins died

Since the moment of God's greatest love of all creation, us got broken
Jesus the breath of God has been picking up our broken pieces of sin
Until the third day when we were breathed back together again

If In Life

Can't help but wonder looking back at what if didn't happen
Would I still have found the gift of writing poetry for the Lord
Or would I have been to distracted doing other desires?

Yes getting cancer or another disease can be dream killers
God takes us through wounds for reasons beyond understanding
But give Him time to heal and teach us His ways make us better

Sometimes life feels stuck trapped in a room, but remember
Some books of the Bible were written inside a tower, in prison
Because they trusted God beyond the words given to be free

Don't know the if in life would have happened like planned
Just like the streams flowing into the river, routes change
While the destination remains the same, which is home

Sometimes God uses us far beyond our wildest imagination
Other times uses us from hospital beds, beyond closed doors
The one thing that will never change is how much God loves us

Those that are humbled before the Lord will be given purpose
That will serve beyond themselves, to who the world can't see
The Kingdom of God is being built from our suffering

God needs the humble to help lead the proud and prideful
He provides the way out of temptation, but doesn't say how
Never said where the window or the door led to next

Paradise Of Jesus

This world is so easy to get lost in that we forget it's not home
We forget Eden was our home till a bite and a lie kicked us out
We've forgotten the shame we felt being left in the dark

Blame God all we want for every foolish thing we've done
Getting mad won't get us out of eating in the pig trough
The prodigal son already returned, now it's our turn

We've gotten so comfortable living in a world we don't belong
Instead of working to get out of the predicament, we unpacked
Making the darkness a place to call home

God's been knocking on the door to tell us He paid for our shame
His sacrifice has shined the way for us to return home finally again
All we have to do is follow His light out of the dark

Staying in shape for the journey home is good, but not for a mirror
Making money to pass on behind is fine, but not to lose the soul
We don't have to impress those that can't see in the dark

Thank you God for the reminders we're to get uncomfortable in darkness
That we're only passing through to be the light walking out of the darkness
So that those still lost know to follow until we see the paradise of Jesus again

Ghost Of Zacchaeus

Opening up the door for the one we love to go through is hard
Never knowing if we'll ever see them again to at least say goodbye
But when it's what they want have to let go

First of four best friends, but we were so close doing everything
Being there for each other in hurt and sorrows even as we'd sleep
For nine years, even at my young age felt like a lifetime

The lasting image from the last time I saw him was opening the door
Never thought in a million years it be the last I would see him again
Not even able to put my best friend to rest

The Ghost of Zacchaeus haunted me for the longest time with guilt
After all it was me that opened up the door, anger inside overwhelmed
But no one taught me how to grieve, so learned to keep things inside

Would life been different if that one moment in time could be done over?
Even if it was to learn how to just say goodbye to be able to lay him to rest
Would I have even understood as a child?

Though life's growing pains hurt so much even as children, God uses us
Age doesn't matter when it comes to grief and helping us mold spiritually
Faith will help us overcome things we may never come to understand

God will give more best friends to comfort, to teach us more about love
Not just any kind of love, but unconditionally that will always forgive wrongs
No matter how much we yell for love to go away, love comes back

The faith grown through life's disappointments helped me understand truth
That funerals won't mean it's the end even for man's best friend, just beginning
With Jesus, yes even Jesus will take Ghost of Zacchaeus to the happy place

Undiagnosed Lyme Disease

Life was going so good, could run and play, explore in the woods
Until all that changed, don't know how or when, just don't remember
My body just started to change with pain to my feet

Loved playing baseball, football with family until I couldn't run
Just couldn't stand, walk like I used too, feet would hurt too much
Saw a foot doctor but did little good for someone full of life

One day started walking when lower legs started tightening
As if stepped into vice grips that turned tighter with each step
Tried explaining best I could, but just sounded like complaints

Biggest pain from undiagnosed Lyme disease isn't physical pain
But the emotional scaring pain of not being believed for so long
What a relief it was to be taken seriously in my shoes

I know everyone hurts, but my pain was more than physical
Only my dogs, my friends that are always there when I needed
Them and the music I listened to gave me places to go in my head

One by one dreams started dying, couldn't pitch in baseball
Shoulders started to hurt, couldn't run, weight was gaining
Other joints were hurting, but was told it was arthritis or tendinitis

Biggest pain from undiagnosed Lyme disease isn't physical pain
But labeled pains, even though trying my hardest to be pleasing
Couldn't do a single chore without needing breaks every 10 minutes

I know everyone hurts and shouldn't complain about my pain
But it wasn't me trying to be lazy, just couldn't do anything long
So I read to dream, listened to music, to dream just getting away

I thank God for the gift of vision inside my head giving me places to go
Just to get away from the pain outside and in needed a place of peace
Little did I know would develop my other gift for writing

Undiagnosed Lyme Diseases (Part 2)

One symptom I rarely mention was my emotional outbursts
Snapped at little things, never in public, but frustrations at home
Would feel so guilty while wondering why I did what I did

Biggest pain from undiagnosed Lyme disease isn't physical
But emotional guilt for lashing out or shaking at those you love
Feeling like a crazy monster was the worst pain of all

Time after time was asked why I acted all angry like at home
Which gave me plenty of time in my closed room to reflect
Couldn't figure out the why, so just talked to God

Year after year, everything got worse, legs quicker to tighten
Forearms tightening kept me from working with my hands
Fingers would go numb from holding the fork too long

Biggest pain from undiagnosed Lyme disease isn't physical
But pain nobody but God can see behind the lonely eyes
Because of inability to explain what I felt walking in my shoes

Wasn't until I got medical assistance since I lost insurance at 18
That finally could start trying to find answers, to my body not working
But by then my weight gaining was too much to be overlooked

Not one doctor gave me answers, just more questions and medication
That caused me to gain more weight, which led to obesity being diagnosed
But was told the rest was me being normal, another false label

Thank God for the dogs he sent me, for speaking to me through music
Writing poetry gave me purpose, peace of mind, even through my pain
Thought it be worth it if I could ease someone else's pain

Undiagnosed Lyme Diseases (Part 3)

Since nobody understood what my body was going through
I just adapted best I could, learned what slowed contractions
Why I only wear shorts, because of tightening on leg contact

Games, TV became my way of escaping so tired of contracting muscles
Food became my medication for emotional frustration and pain relief
Not being able to exercise, weight became even more of a burden

Stuttering didn't help, just another label, a confidence stealer
Another symptom that gets own referral for speech therapy
Nobody thought to add symptoms up or put them together

Getting diabetes became more of a blessing than a burden
Helped me to read labels in eating better, result of losing weight
But didn't matter what I'd lose, eventually gain all back

Golf was the only thing keeping me from going crazy
Gave me an outlet for frustrations, something I could do
Thank God for golf carts so I didn't walk until feet went numb

Through all the years God has been good to me, providing needs
Helping my faith get stronger with every broken, pained step taken
Speaking words of poetry for me to write

After all these years of undiagnosed, 1000 prayers said for healing
God provided the way using my Uncle's wedding to see my Great Cousin
Who gave me what no doctor has given me, right diagnosis, answers to pain

Took 24 years to find it's been parasites all these years of Lyme disease
Part of me wants to be angry, but the faith in me knows it was God's plan
Like He used the thorn in the side of Apostle Paul

KYLE WALKER

Don't know how long the road to recovery will take me, don't know the stops
But I look forward to what God has to give me along the way to being healed
With one faithful step at a time will get there

Looking back with all the people I've touched, books of poetry written
Don't know if I'd want anything changed not even the pain felt inside
Because it's what God used to help me make a difference

God has been so faithful, watching every step I take, so I don't fall
Providing every dog I've needed to remind me to be calm, be still
God is watching so do not worry He will provide to do His will

Biggest pain from undiagnosed Lyme disease isn't physical
But it doesn't matter anymore because God's grace is enough
Who needs normal, all we need is humility and His love

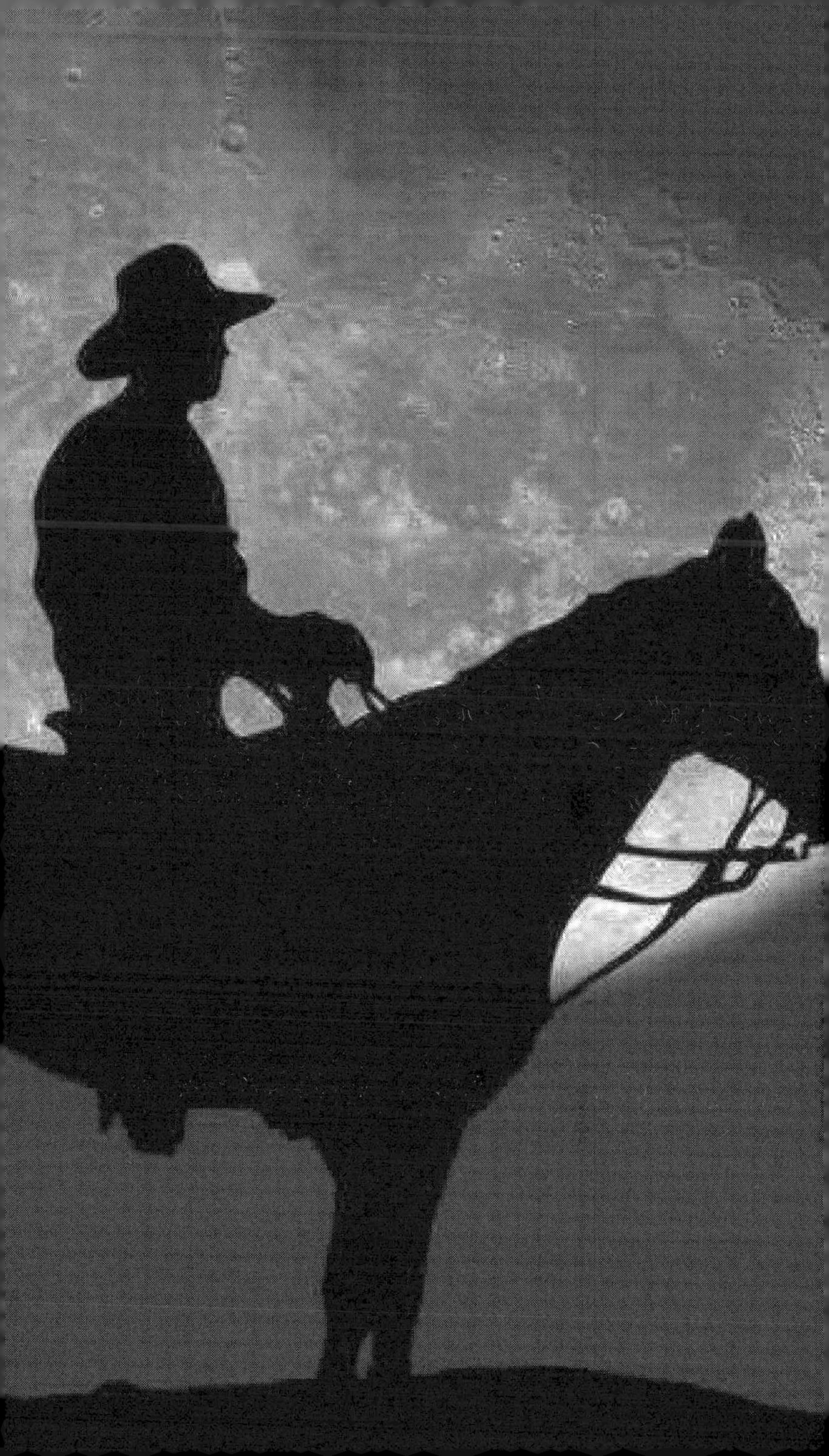

Coming of Dawn, The Signs Of Time

Only have to wait few more hours till the coming of dawn
Even though the pain felt through night has been tormenting
The separation between darkness and light is soon over

Before the beginning of time God and darkness was it until
God spoke let there be light and creation was breathed life
Then came the 6th day when we were born from dust

Far too long we have made darkness our bed, shame our pillow
Crying our self pity, instead of crying out to God in repentance
But our pride keeps us from accepting His love for us

Living in paradise we were Adam and Eve with no darkness in sight
Until the bite turned out the light, leaving us naked in the night
Giving birth into sin with an endless generation of no innocence

Signs of the times, thanks to the Lord for working His perfection
The sacrifice of His life, for our sins on the cross gave us a rebirth
He raised us up from the darkness of death into the light of life

If only we'd stop living like we're dead with sin blocking the Light
Tormenting our souls with the guilt of unrepented sin to Christ
All the while time keeps counting past midnight until His return

Pre-dawning is upon us the Son's light is overpowering the dark
The sorrows will be leaving our hearts, shame felt be gone for good
His grace turned the light back on like the bite never happened

Except for those refusing to repent so their sins could be forgiven
They never believed, they couldn't stop trying to earn the way back
If only they listened to the signs of time that Jesus was the only Son

Midnight Ride Of The Son

Let there be light God said then separated darkness from light
The first midnight ride began of the sun to the coming of dawn
Was all for fun until the darkness of satan started playing for keeps

While we're praying our souls to keep before we sleep, He listens
Then He speaks while saddling up for His midnight ride to save us
If we listen before turning out the lights we can hear Him

Sacrificing on the altar used to be the only signal for the Midnight rider
The blood on the doorposts was the sign for our debts have been paid
But that wasn't enough so He used His blood on a cross for all of time

Between the sun and the moon it's the way time has always been
No storm cloud has hidden the truth even when our eyes can't see
The Midnight Rider racing against time to save until the last soul

For over 2,000 years the Midnight Rider has been watching over us
Catching every tear, healing every heartache till we feel His love enough
So we'd cry out to Him, believing He's the Son of God that saved us

What we don't know is that the Midnight Rider listens for the last soul
And when the last soul cries out to be saved it will be the last midnight ride
Because the sun and the moon will be replaced by His glory

Paul Revere was a midnight rider that warned the British were coming
Well Jesus, our Midnight Rider, rides to warn He's coming if we listen
Those that listen will be saved on His midnight ride before last sunrise

Can we hear Him? I hear Him calling my name as He races to save me
Don't let the dead of night stop you, stop me from catching a ride with
The Midnight Rider, the Son of God, saving the last soul, is it you? Or me?

Mamma Read To Me

Thank you Mamma for reading to me, to us before sleep
For showing us it's okay to dream even when so young
Whether it's the Good Book or a book of poetry

One poem down only the Author knows how many more to go
Not even I know, guess long as His Spirit keeps speaking to me
I will keep writing to inspire you girls to read to your children

Thank you Mamma for reading to your children before bed
Should feel blessed by raising them to be women of God
And if my poetry had some part inspiring then I am humbled

Even if it's one more poem to go before book's end keep reading
The next one God willing soon be done, hopefully in time for bed
If not know God will always speak through you with love to pass on

Thank you Mamma for not giving up, for delivering God's plans
Just like He delivered you to raise His kingdom's princesses
Like you, they will read to their children as they remember you

About The Author

Kyle Walker is the author of five books of poetry. Self taught, he uses his life experiences to glorify God, and hopes to inspire his readers to reflect on God's love as they read his works.

Made in the USA
Charleston, SC
19 September 2016